A SCHOOL LEADER'S GUIDE TO LEADING PROFESSIONAL DEVELOPMENT

Continuing professional development can be a powerful force in any school improvement programme, leading to better student outcomes and making recruitment and staff retention easier. *A School Leader's Guide to Leading Professional Development* provides an effective and evidence-based approach to creating a culture of continuous learning in schools.

Covering all aspects of CPD including teacher quality, what CPD looks like and how it should develop over time, creating an inspirational culture, CPD design, coaching, and much more, the chapters encourage readers to reflect on how they are currently using CPD and how this could be improved. Appendices provide templates and charts to use in the planning of CPD sessions, as well as questions to guide sessions and evaluations with participants on an individual and whole-school level.

Based on the author's experience of implementing CPD programmes as a school leader, well-regarded trainer, and now the head of a leading international educational consultancy, this is essential reading for school leaders wanting to create a 'culture of learning' in their school and among their teachers.

Costa Constantinou is a former school leader and director of education at Veema Education, a leading CPD provider.

A SCHOOL LEADER'S GUIDE TO LEADING PROFESSIONAL DEVELOPMENT

Costa Constantinou

LONDON AND NEW YORK

Designed cover image: © Getty Images

First published 2025
by Routledge
4 Park Square, Milton Park, Abingdon, Oxon OX14 4RN

and by Routledge
605 Third Avenue, New York, NY 10158

Routledge is an imprint of the Taylor & Francis Group, an informa business

© 2025 Costa Constantinou

The right of Costa Constantinou to be identified as author of this work has been asserted in accordance with sections 77 and 78 of the Copyright, Designs and Patents Act 1988.

All rights reserved. No part of this book may be reprinted or reproduced or utilised in any form or by any electronic, mechanical, or other means, now known or hereafter invented, including photocopying and recording, or in any information storage or retrieval system, without permission in writing from the publishers.

Trademark notice: Product or corporate names may be trademarks or registered trademarks, and are used only for identification and explanation without intent to infringe.

British Library Cataloguing-in-Publication Data
A catalogue record for this book is available from the British Library

Library of Congress Cataloging-in-Publication Data
Names: Constantinou, Costa, author.
Title: A school leader's guide to leading professional development / Costa Constantinou.
Description: Abingdon, Oxon ; New York, NY : Routledge, 2025. | Includes bibliographical references and index.
Identifiers: LCCN 2024027874 (print) | LCCN 2024027875 (ebook) | ISBN 9781032140582 (hardback) | ISBN 9781032140599 (paperback) | ISBN 9781003232179 (ebook)
Subjects: LCSH: Teachers–In-service training–Planning. | School management and organization. | School environment.
Classification: LCC LB1731 .C6326 2025 (print) | LCC LB1731 (ebook) | DDC 370.71/55–dc23/eng/20240806
LC record available at https://lccn.loc.gov/2024027874
LC ebook record available at https://lccn.loc.gov/2024027875

ISBN: 978-1-032-14058-2 (hbk)
ISBN: 978-1-032-14059-9 (pbk)
ISBN: 978-1-003-23217-9 (ebk)

DOI: 10.4324/9781003232179

Typeset in Interstate
by Apex CoVantage, LLC

I dedicate this book to all the wonderful school leaders and teachers who are doing their best to be excellent educators at a time when the teaching profession is facing significant challenges.

And, of course, to Murat Kaya, Lisa Jane Ashes, and all my brilliant colleagues who have shaped and continue to shape my career. Thank you.

Costa

CONTENTS

About the Author — xii

1 Introduction: 13 Weeks Holiday and Home by Four — 1

My Past, Shaping My Future — 1
Teacher Training — 2
About This Book — 5
Making the Most of This Book — 6
Putting People First — 7
Reflective Questions — 8

2 Teacher Quality: Why It Matters — 9

What Are Experts, and Why Do We Need Them? — 9
The Problem With Change — 14
The Culture of Plateaus — 16
Culture a Real Game Changer — 16
Becoming a Cultural Leader — 17
Professional Environments Matter! — 19
Before We Conclude, a Cautionary Note to Be 'Critical Consumers' — 22
Conclusion — 24
Reflective Questions — 24
Chapter Snapshots — 25
References — 26

3 Ensuring CPD Is Effective and Avoiding Common Pitfalls — 29

Effective Professional Development (PD) — 31
How Do We Do This? — 32

viii Contents

    What Makes Effective Professional Development:
       EEF Guidance, 2021   36
    Six Deadly Errors to Avoid When Planning Your
       Professional Development   41
    Conclusion   45
    Reflective Questions   45
    Chapter Snapshots   46
    References   47

4 Habits of Great Leaders That Work in Times of Crisis and Give Us Time to Improve   48

    Skills of an Agile Leader   49
    Habit Formation and Behaviour Change   53
    Developing Teachers Through Purposeful Practice   53
    The Power of Tiny Habits Over Long Periods of Time   56
    The Four Laws of Behaviour Change   57
    Leading Effective CPD: Applying the Rider and
       Elephant Analogy to Our Work   62
    The Power of Motivation to Sustain Good Habits   63
    Keeping Everyone on Track   65
    The Impact of Dopamine on Human Motivation   66
    But . . . Dopamine Isn't the Only Chemical We Need   67
    Creating 'Thinking' Environments   67
    Tweaking the School Environment to
       Support Professional Learning   69
    The Four Stages of Competence by Noel Burch   71
    Conclusion   73
    Reflective Questions   74
    Chapter Snapshots   74
    References   76

5 How to Plan and Deliver Effective Teacher CPD   77

    Five Vital Musts   78
    Teacher Appreciation of Your Session   82
    Delivery Methods   83

Simplified CPD: Frameworks for Effortless Planning and Deliver	84
What Makes a Great CPD Programme?	86
INSET Days: Making Every Moment Count!	90
Professional Development Sessions, Twilights, and Teachmeets	93
Online CPD	96
Educational Conferences	98
Demystifying CPD Delivery: Avoiding Logistical Nightmares	99
Overcoming Common Difficulties in Leading Whole-School CPD	101
Dealing With Challenging Individuals	102
Conclusion	106
Reflective Questions	106
Chapter Snapshots	107
References	108

6 Enhancing CPD Through Effective Coaching — 110

Exploring Principles and Practices	111
Who Should Coach?	114
Transactional Analysis and Coaching	114
Teacher Collaboration	116
Coaching for Effective CPD	118
Fostering Strong Coaching Relationships – My Five Golden Principles	120
Questioning for Personal Growth	122
Types of Questions	122
Reflection on Coaching Questions	123
Effective Questioning Is Rooted in Attentive Listening	123
Instructional Coaching	126
Meaningful Lesson Observations	132
Addressing Barriers to Instructional Coaching	135
Conclusion	137
Reflective Questions	137
Chapter Snapshots	138
References	139

7 The Evaluation of Continuous Professional Development — 141

Let's Pause! — 141
Great Professional Development That Leads to Great Pedagogy — 144
Standard for Teachers' Professional Development — 147
What Is Evaluation? — 148
Applying Guskey's Five Critical Levels of Professional Development Evaluation — 160
Planning Effective CPD Evaluations — 165
Paradigm Shift — 165
Conclusion — 166
Reflective Questions — 167
Chapter Snapshots — 167
References — 168

8 Conclusion — 170

The Case for High-Quality CPD — 172
The Key Message — 173
Successfully Designing and Planning Good CPD — 174
Their Opinion Has Not Been Taken Into Account — 176

Appendices — 183
Appendix 1: Case Study — 185
Appendix 2: Reflecting on Professional Development — 189
  Whole-School Professional Development Plan — 190
Appendix 3: PAUSE FOR THOUGHT – Agile Leadership Quick Reference — 191
Appendix 4: Planning Your Safeguarding Training: Guidance for Annual and Termly Training Example — 192
Appendix 5: Lesson Observation Template: Generating Understanding and Raising Awareness — 193
Appendix 6 — 194

Appendix 7: Level 1 – Participants' Reactions Evaluation
Questionnaire – Example Template 196
Appendix 8: Level 2 – Participants' Learning
Evaluation Questionnaire 198
Appendix 9: Interview Questions (Post-Training) 199
Appendix 10: Example Timeframe for Carrying Out a
CPD Evaluation 203
Appendix 11: CPD Audit Checklist 205
Index 208

ABOUT THE AUTHOR

Costa Constantinou cofounded Veema in 2013 after a long teaching career in London. He is driven by his passionate belief in the transformative power of education to create opportunities. Growing up in a migrant family, Costa embraced the significance of schooling from an early age. Having been deprived of education, his parents instilled a deep appreciation for learning.

Costa understands firsthand the needs and priorities of schools today. He has led national and international keynotes and workshops on improving teaching and learning, school leadership, and implementing and managing effective change. Costa passionately advocates that professional development is a requisite tool for teachers to engage with pedagogy, offer collaborative working partnerships, and challenge and advance existing practices. Taken together, these sharpen our ability to focus on how we teach and how pupils learn - a reflective approach that, at its core, sees learning through the eyes of the learner.

Veema's professional development and school improvement programmes empower teachers and school leaders worldwide, fostering continuous learning for the benefit of their students.

1 Introduction
13 Weeks Holiday and Home by Four

My Past, Shaping My Future

It's Thursday, January 27, 2022, 4 pm, and I can't quite believe I'm actually doing this!

I've finally sat down and written the first paragraph of this book … my book.

It's taken me some time to start, and I know it will take me some time to finish not just because I have so much to share (having worked in so many schools around the world) but also because writing has never come easy to me. I have dyslexia. Growing up, I was the kid that received additional school-based interventions for literacy. I was the child that needed my teachers to know how to reach me through their skill and knowledge. I needed teachers who had been trained well and used that training to help me access the education that would shape my future.

Over the years, I have developed my own coping strategies so my dyslexia has not held me back. My teachers could have provided those strategies much earlier; if they had, I may have finished this book with ease! I was successful **despite** dyslexia. How many children have not been so lucky? My negative experiences of education became a driver for me. I want students to avoid having to figure out how to access education because their teachers are trained to provide them with the key.

My drive came from my parents. My parents grew up in Cyprus, from similar backgrounds. Both were poor and, in their own ways, were deprived of education. My father, for instance, was taken out of primary school to work with my grandfather (Pappou), a local fisherman, because school was seen as secondary when you have nine in the family to feed.

As for my mother, she left high school at age 13 when her father passed away. And because the family could no longer survive financially in Cyprus, my mother's older brother, who was already in the UK, brought her and her seven younger siblings along with my grandfather and grandmother (Yiayia) to England.

My mum was an A-star student, and she'd been promised, I'm told, that she could continue her schooling in the UK, but once she reached London, she was sent to work as a seamstress at a clothing factory owned by Greek Cypriots. Again, providing money for the family took precedence over her dreams of going to university.

While my parents lost out on education, they never lost sight of its importance and so they turned their sights to their children. Like many migrants coming to the UK in the 1960s (and still today), both my parents worked hard to make sure I and my three sisters were never without and, more importantly, that we went to school and worked towards university. This meant doing well academically became ingrained in our DNA.

As they saw it, education was the Willy Wonka ticket we needed for a better life.

My passionate belief in equality and inclusivity and my love for teaching stem from the values my parents instilled in me from a young age and the sacrifices my parents made to ensure their children had the best possible education. Now, I get to work with schools worldwide to ensure that their students get the best possible education (despite any specific learning difficulties or a lack of inspirational parenting). I see the opportunities schools have to grow much in the same way that my parents looked at their children. No matter what starting point students come to you from, they can be led to successful futures by highly skilled, highly trained teachers ... if we get their professional development right!

Teacher Training

Even before I was accepted to study a PGCE in 2003 in humanities and social sciences at the Institute of Education (IOE), I just knew teaching was right for me. I loved the idea of working with young people and supporting them towards great futures, just as my parents did for me. I must admit to naively thinking that 13 weeks of holiday a year wasn't a bad perk too. I was quickly put right about what teaching was all about. On day two of our course, Mary, our PGCE tutor and a strong-minded Northerner, told us three truths about teaching, the first of many pearls of wisdom that she dropped into our ears over the terms that followed.

Number one: 'Don't think your day will end at four because it won't.'
Number two: 'If you don't enjoy working with children, then this isn't the job for you.'
Number three: 'Do not become a teacher just for the holidays.'

Perish the thought.

I vividly remember the first time I taught a lesson. It was Year 10, religious studies. My mentor introduced me and then suddenly left the classroom, leaving me to fend for myself. I recall seeing 30 sets of eyes looking at me, waiting for me to do something. It was definitely one of those sink-and-swim moments, and lucky for me, the outcome was a positive one. (I'm not sure the students felt the same.) My confidence got me through, but my mentor should have made sure it was a learning experience for me. How we educate our teachers is so important for their outcome. What if it had not gone well? Would I have given up on teaching and found a different suit to wear? This happens to far too many new recruits in the profession, and part of my mission is to support all teachers to stay and find their best.

Pause for a Moment!

What do you remember from the first-ever lesson you taught as a new teacher?
What did you learn? What did you need from your mentors back then?
Do you provide your newer staff with that support? How? Why?

Despite my abandonment experience in the early days of teaching, I was lucky enough to move forward and work with two exceptional heads of department and the humanities who led me in a far more developmental way as a fledgling teacher. They were creative, innovative, and showed me how high-quality teaching can impact the lives of our students. The students loved the humanities subjects. At one point, we had over 70 students studying A-level RS. It was so humbling to be a part of a brilliant team. At the time, I didn't fully realise the impact this was having on me as a teacher and leader. Looking back at my mentors, I can now see the steps to my success. My mentors were passionate about their subject; they wanted the children to love the subject and showed me how to do this too. They were always engaged in my progress and provided specific feedback for my development. They were focused upon my actions and not my personality, which always made the feedback easier to take. In this book, I want to make these steps (and many others) visible for leaders so that we can emulate them, not by accident, purposefully to develop our own great teachers.

As a result of such excellent leaders, early in my teaching career, I wanted to start influencing whole-school decision-making. I began the ascent, climbing the career ladder. Becoming head of year in my third year of teaching meant I had more responsibility for pastoral care, something I absolutely love and had long been interested in. However, looking after the emotional and academic welfare of over 240 students is a big job. And yes, there were times that I got it wrong, but thankfully, I had excellent colleagues around me, and this, along with the professional development I received, allowed me to excel. In these early years, I was also studying for a master's degree in social justice and education. This qualification gave me the foundations I needed to put theory into practice. Each step upon that ladder has led to new learning, new experiences, and new ways of working that can often be invisible at the time. I became involved in professional development following my leadership pathways qualification from the National College. I had a thirst for learning and getting better (some things suffered in my personal life, I must admit), but I was trying to improve as a teacher and leader. Like many of us, when I got to leadership, I realised that one area I had control over during the school day was when I was in the classroom with my students. This was the only time

I could not be disturbed, so my focus was always on making sure that my lessons were well-planned. And my students got the best out of me, and I got the best out of them. I tried very hard to always commit to this, even if it meant lesson planning over the weekend. The way I managed my week was to always plan my lessons up to Wednesday so I knew exactly what I was doing. This helped me breathe and gave me space to handle my other responsibilities. I would never say you must work on weekends, but in reality, most of us do, which, I hate to say, was what worked for me. I compensated for this mentally by committing to rest and fully switching off during half-terms and other holidays

All of this has shaped who I am today as an educator and as a person. I have evaluated my experiences then and now and provided the best for you here in this book.

About This Book

Improving teachers' professional development leads to a better education experience for all. All students deserve the best possible chance in life; education needs to be excellent! It is for this reason that designing and delivering highly impactful professional development to schools around the world has dominated the last nine years of my professional career.

Throughout this book, I aim to share the best insights gained from a wide array of school systems, curriculums, and cultures. The goal is to support you in developing the most effective continuing professional development (CPD) programmes possible. Each chapter is designed to give you pause for thought and stimulate your thinking. I've explored various elements crucial for planning and delivering professional development, drawing from educational evidence on effective CPD and non-educational literature that guides successful change and professional growth in our organisations. It's similar to baking the perfect chocolate brownie – every ingredient matters, along with the time it takes to cook.

I have covered topics that are important, drawing from both my own experience and valuable research on what makes effective CPD for teachers. These include insights into the habits of great leaders, strategies for planning and delivering various types of CPD, the importance of follow-up through coaching and mentoring, and diverse approaches to evaluating CPD in schools.

This is an investment, and reshaping our perspective on professional development in schools can't rely on a single individual. It must be ingrained in the core culture of the school, forming an integral part of the school system designed to facilitate change. Blaming colleagues for a lack of investment in professional development is only worthwhile if we provide them with time, space, or structured training with a clear starting and end point.

If you believe, as I do, that education is a basic human right of a child and that every school must work strategically to provide the highest level of education. If you know that teaching always has more potential, and with proper training, the learning imparted has the potential to be accessed by all students. If you are aware that teachers are the key to our student's success and really want to improve the professional development of your school, then you are really going to enjoy this book.

Making the Most of This Book

In each chapter, you will be encouraged to reflect on your current position with the ideas presented on professional development – where you are now and where you aspire to be. Each chapter provides frameworks to support your work and offers ways to strategically plan professional development or fine-tune certain aspects of CPD in your school that you know need improving. Whether your goal is to enhance the quality of CPD in a specific part of your school, department/faculty, or the entire school, I hope that the book will provide you with lots of practical ideas and the research evidence you need to engage you and your colleagues in this process and get you to where you need to be.

You may wish to focus more on a particular chapter that addresses an area you are working on improving in your school, for example, 'the evaluation CPD.' If this is the case, don't overlook other chapters where I have referenced connections and common threads.

As a reader, I'd ask you to use this book to support your work, initiate the changes you'd like to make, find substantial evidence to support this direction, and discover ideas to design and implement effective teacher-learning environments with high-quality professional development.

At the end of each chapter, I have included a set of reflection questions that you can use for thinking. I find questions like these to be a good way to open up dialogues with colleagues, so I encourage you to share them as you see fit. Additionally, short, guided questions like these every two or three weeks can initiate change in any aspect of our schools and conversation starters.

Whether you read this book as a headteacher, CPD leader, lead practitioner, or simply after inspirational CPD ideas to 'jazz' up what you are already doing, there's much to delve into, including the resources in the appendices. Offering quality CPD establishes the foundation for prioritising teacher learning and investing in people for the benefit of our students. It also instils a sense of accountability that all teachers in our schools need to embrace and improve over the years. This common thread is referred to often throughout the book

Putting People First

Despite what some might say about teaching and what the media may write, we all know that teachers don't come into the profession for the holidays or because they want to be home by four; I don't know many teachers in the UK who leave school before five or do not work at home. We work long hours and battle a workload that never diminishes. I want to draw attention to this burden because it is one of the key reasons teachers leave our profession. That, of course, is a great shame because it means many talented people are having to make tough choices, especially when the teaching profession desperately needs to provide more educational and pastoral support to children post-pandemic; our schools must be safe places not only for our students but also for their families and other teachers where there is an even greater need for pastoral care post-COVID. We play such a big role in our community through the support we provide our young people both academically and personally. We are the rock others need to be successful.

We need to think of our teachers as more than a teacher of English, a teacher of math, or a teacher of history. Yes, we may be academic experts, but increasingly, our roles are expanding to facilitators, social workers, psychologists, mental health ambassadors, and surrogate parents. In modern society, many of the young people we teach need more from us than just the academic. If we get our professional development programme right, we can provide our young people with everything they need. With such great responsibility should come even greater professional development for those who choose to remain. As a leader of professional development, you need to recognise your teachers' reality and provide development that keeps them in the profession and gives them the tools and knowledge they need to traverse the ever-changing landscape of education with as much ease as possible.

I hope you will enjoy this book and find the ideas and strategies useful in improving the professional development at your school.

Reflective Questions

1. What part of my story can you relate to?
2. What type of professional development has had the largest impact on you so far?
3. What would teachers in your school say about the CPD (continuing professional development) in your school?
4. Does your school support your views on professional development and staff development?
5. How do you manage your own workload and encourage others to do the same?
6. What evidence do you use to support staff in managing their workload?
7. How do you balance professional development to ensure it is not burdensome for staff?
8. What do you do to prioritise people over exam results and school policies?

2 Teacher Quality
Why It Matters

'If you keep doing what you've been doing, you'll keep getting what you've been getting.' Susan Jeffers' book 'Feel the Fear and Do It Anyway' (2007) gave me this mantra. It captures concisely the truth that change is a necessary component in all walks of life (especially when the world is transforming so fast). As school leaders, we know this only too well. If we do not provide teachers with high-quality professional development (including access to good resources, colleagues, and adequate time to improve), then change will be slow. We should look to build an environment where a willingness to embrace change is simply part of everyday school life.

Back when I was an NQT, I remember my deputy head saying, 'No matter how many years you've been teaching, Costa, you will always look to do things differently. When we care, we can always do things better.' If I were to try and identify the moment that set me off down the CPD path, this would probably be it.

In this chapter, I want us to explore the following:

- Teacher quality
- How teacher quality affects a school
- How teacher quality affects its students
- How we can improve teacher quality

What Are Experts, and Why Do We Need Them?

As Figure 2.1 illustrates, teachers are the most powerful influencers on pupil achievement. Great teachers play a pivotal role in student achievement. Read through the list provided in Figure 2.1. Where do

DOI: 10.4324/9781003232179-2

you currently focus your interventions for improving teaching and learning? Expertise doesn't always develop over time; colleagues who tell us that they are experts because they have been doing it for years can be narrow in their thinking. They have been practising in one way for a long time. They are good at it. They may have picked up bad habits, and through a lack of wider research, they don't even realise that they are bad. An expert can take a wider view of their topic of expertise through research, learning, trial and error, observing others, and finding new ways. Time does not always mean an expert has been formed. It is our deliberate practice that leads us to becoming experts.

There is a wide consensus that teachers have the most significant influence on student academic progress. For instance, Hattie's (2008) work on visible learning highlights teacher's positive impact on student achievement. We also know that students taught by expert teachers are up to three times more likely to achieve compared to those who receive tuition from novice teachers. In other words, teachers are the most valuable resource schools have in terms of raising student standards.

Knowing that our teachers are the source of student achievement means that the question 'How can I help my teachers improve?' is one of the most important questions any school leader can ask themselves.

It is no coincidence that the top-performing schools focus a lot of energy on the improvement of classroom teaching. They also invest in tools to help them achieve this. McKinsey's 2007 report, 'How the World's Best-Performing School Systems Come Out on Top' (Barber and Mourshed, 2007), makes for some interesting reading on this topic. From the 25 countries studied in this report, they found that the highest-performing institutions focus most on upgrading teaching quality and providing teachers with the resources needed to be effective educators.

Pause for Reflection

While considering these questions, jot down your answers and come back to them later:

- Are you using research from sources such as the McKinsey report to inform your decisions?

Teacher Quality

- What are you doing now to invest in teacher quality improvement?
- What tools do you have in place to support your teachers to improve their quality?
- What plans do you have in place to ensure that teacher quality is of the highest importance in your school?

Expert teachers are those who know how to present and teach subject material using the most appropriate pedagogical methods for

Influence	Effect Size	Source of Influence
Feedback	1.13	Teacher
Students' prior cognitive ability	1.04	Student
Instructional quality	1.00	Teacher
Direct instruction	.82	Teacher
Remediation/feedback	.65	Teacher
Students' disposition to learn	.61	Student
Class environment	.56	Teacher
Challenge of goals	.52	Teacher
Peer tutoring	.50	Teacher
Mastery learning	.50	Teacher
Parent involvement	.46	**Home**
Homework	.43	Teacher
Teacher style	.42	Teacher
Questioning	.41	Teacher
Peer effects	.38	**Peers**
Advance organisers	.37	Teacher
Simulation and games	.34	Teacher
Computer-assisted instruction	.31	Teacher
Testing	.30	Teacher
Instructional media	.30	Teacher
Aims and policy of the school	.24	school
Affective attributes of students	.24	Student
Physical attributes of students	.21	Student
Programmed instruction	.18	Teacher
Ability grouping	.18	School
Audio-visual aids	.16	Teacher
Individualisation	.14	Teacher
Finances/money	.12	School
Behavioural objectives	.12	Teacher
Team teaching	.06	Teacher
Physical attributes (e.g., class size)	-.05	School
Television	-.12	**Home**
Retention	-.15	School

Figure 2.1 Adapted from Hattie, John, 'Teachers Make a Difference, What is the research evidence?' (2003), https://research.acer.edu.au/research_conference_2003/4

the students in front of them at any given time. In their lessons, they foster a learning environment that enables them to develop excellent relationships with their students. They also spend time getting better at their craft by deepening their already excellent subject knowledge and continuously thinking about how they can improve their own classroom practice. They read the latest research and practise deliberately to put the research into reality. All of this is underpinned by an unshakeable belief that those they teach can achieve success.

Although this is open to interpretation, I feel the ideas included in the following list provide us with some good points for discussion:

We Tend to Agree on the Following Regarding Expert Teachers:

- Present and teach subject material in the most effective way.
- Have excellent subject knowledge and use the right pedagogical approach to support successful learning.
- Expert teachers display a profound pedagogical awareness of teaching and learning.
- Monitor learning and provide feedback.
- Foster a unique learning culture and develop excellent relationships with students.
- Believe all students can reach the success criteria.
- Are continuously reflective and think about their classroom practice and how this can be improved.

Perhaps there is more to add to this list. Expert teachers embark on an endless journey of discovery and learning, and I include myself in this endeavour. When recruiting new staff, I always ask, 'How has this teacher recently advanced their professional practice?' This inquiry reveals a great deal about a person's attitude, mindset, and commitment to continuous learning. I seek to hire teachers who understand that we are never a finished product. As long as we are teaching, there is always more to learn.

How do we get the highest quality teachers?

Through effective continuous professional development (CPD), teachers can enhance their practice and improve their teaching skills, enthusing them to want to grow even more. Of course, we need buy-in from teachers, and teachers must understand that there is a commitment on their part to invest in their own professional development journey, just as we are investing in them. We improve not just for ourselves but also for those around us and, of course, for our students. This culture needs to be firmly rooted from the ground up in our schools, and only when we do this can we develop an excellent culture of professional learning. In my experience, when our teachers adopt this mindset, our students will do so too.

How schools help teachers improve their skills is particularly important in the landscape in which I am writing this (post-pandemic). We already know from the Education Endowment Foundation's 'The Impact of COVID-19 on Learning: A Review of the Evidence' (2022) that there has been a significant decline in student attainment, specifically among disadvantaged groups and younger learners. I'm sure the actual measured impact will continue to grow as more studies are carried out. Teachers are required to fill the lost learning gaps, so they must be supported to develop their skills to match this new learning crisis. The crisis of the future is not yet known. However, with this most recent crisis so soon in our memories, we must see that having teachers with adaptive skills is crucial. Teachers who are trained properly and who are properly motivated to seek to develop their practice are the teachers we need when things go wrong.

Every teacher can be that teacher ... as long as they have excellent CPD.

From the outset, the title of this chapter, 'Teacher Quality - Why It Matters,' might seem obvious, but the research evidence is telling us that we still have a long way to go. So far, despite many government policies such as the DfE's initiatives and the work of organisations such as the Teacher Development Trust and Chartered College of Teaching in the UK, teacher retention rates and recruitment remain at an all-time low and are getting worse. The latest initial teacher training statistics published show that only 59% of the target for secondary schools was met in 2022-2023, down from 79% in the previous year.

You probably have experience with this at your own school when it comes to recruiting and retaining staff. The question is, What are we doing about this?

1. Attract good practitioners.
2. Retain good practitioners.
3. Enable good practitioners to share their expertise with others.

Recruiting the best!

We need to successfully attract more teachers into the profession and then really invest in their professional development. At the time of writing this book, things are not looking good for teacher recruitment in the UK. There are so many external factors as to why teacher recruitment and retention rates are at an all-time low in the UK. Some factors are within our control as school leaders. Providing excellent professional development and the proper support and care will lead to a higher sense of achievement and a feeling of value. We can get this right!

The Problem With Change

Unfortunately, bringing about change is not easy given the difficulty of changing habits in both pupils and staff, what we can call **'personal inertia.'** It's well-known, and as Rivkin, Hanushek and Kain (2005) have shown, improvements in a teacher's skills can often flatline after the first couple of years. I think Joshua Foer (2012) described this aspect very well in his book 'Moonwalking with Einstein' when he talks of the period when we no longer seek to achieve greater expertise but are satisfied with just being able to perform basic skills on autopilot as the '**OK plateau**.' He used it to describe that common autopilot state when you have habitually mastered the basics of a task, but despite being skilled, you stop improving before you reach expert status; you simply plateau in performance. Teachers are as prone to this state as any other profession. It is crucial to think about how this can be avoided.

The questions we need to consider here are as follows:

- Is this the type of language we regularly use in our school to ensure it's not perceived as a weakness or even insulting staff?

- What does this really look like in the classroom?
- How do we develop high-quality teaching practitioners who keep getting better in our school?

Perhaps the answer starts with addressing the type of professional development teachers have been exposed to. Maybe this lack of introspection is one of the reasons why teacher quality can often flatline after the first couple of years. And this is something you, as a school leader, must always be fighting against. How can you move on from this point of inertia to ensure teaching practitioners keep getting better?

First, ask: What do you already do? By examining the teacher training you are already providing, determine whether it is sufficient to bring about the change and improvements we have talked about. Are you using research like the McKinsey report mentioned at the start of this chapter on high-performing schools to inform your own decision-making?

Second, ask: What is possible? By making available to teaching staff (at every level) the very best professional development that enables them to become subject experts committed to evidence-informed and experiential practice.

Unfortunately, despite mounting evidence about the importance of improving teacher quality, many CPD training programmes don't offer real benefits to either teaching professionals or their schools. The type of professional development most teachers are exposed to – one-off training INSETS, seminars, and workshops – barely scratches the surface when we are looking at developing expert teaching.

And third, ask: How do we keep this momentum moving forward? The answer seems clear to me and includes giving teachers the time to 'sharpen the sword,' as Stephen Covey (2020) put it. This means allowing teachers to step back from their classroom commitments and giving them structured time with more expert practitioners to problem-solve and talk about their teaching and pedagogy.

Do you have an organised structure for more experienced teachers to work with and pass on their knowledge and expertise to new teachers coming into your school?

The 'knowing-doing gap' also comes to mind, as discussed by Jeffrey Pfeffer and Robert I. Sutton (2000) in another excellent book. We need to emphasise the importance of action. Providing teachers with knowledge is insufficient and will not improve their practice unless we offer them the opportunities to apply it over time and engage in self-analysis.

The Culture of Plateaus

How do we avoid this 'OK plateau' that is so damaging to the achievement of our young learners? For me, this is very important. If we are going to keep getting better at what we do, then we need create a climate that enables others to grow where we provide the right resources for them to do this and a culture that, as teachers, we keep getting better.

One of which is addressing 'school culture.' Happy people stay in organisations where they feel supported, are able to excel professionally, and feel part of the school improvement journey. Teachers are by far the most important resource in our schools. Therefore, creating a culture where teachers feel invested in and where they are involved in their professional development journey are key areas we should be thinking about when looking at how we are developing staff. They deserve this, and it is our moral duty as leaders to make this a high priority.

Culture a Real Game Changer

You've probably heard the expression often attributed to leadership consultant Peter Drucker that 'culture eats strategy for breakfast.' It's true. It does. No matter what a school leader might want to do, our plans will always be derailed at some point by the behaviours, characteristics, customs, language, systems, assumptions, beliefs, and written and unwritten rules embedded within a school. Or 'this is the way we do things here.'

Culture creates the conditions that enable everyone to flourish, grow, and become better at what they do. Or not. Culture can have a massive impact, good or bad, in areas such as staff retention. Happy people, for instance, stay in organisations where they feel supported, can excel professionally, and where they feel part of the school's improvement journey. In contrast, when that's not there, they move on.

As school leaders, we should ensure the right culture emerges in the first place and is then carefully nurtured. This is a tough task for even the best and almost impossible for those without the necessary leadership skills, but this task can't be avoided.

One factor that will have a disproportionate impact on the culture of any organisation, educational or otherwise, is the level of trust that is found there. You cannot build a strong culture, one that is supportive of learning, without high levels of trust running into every corner and crevice of a school. If there is no clear message from the leadership team that trust should be an essential component of every element of school life, then little progress will be made in creating the positive culture that's needed.

If you want to improve levels of trust within your school, or any organisation for that matter, then I'd say start by reading Steven Covey and Rebecca Merrill's book 'The Speed of Trust' (2008). In it, Covey argues trust should be the number one competency issue for leaders because of its potential to bring out the best in people.

In high-trust organisations, for instance, more productive environments develop because people find it easier to break out of their comfort zones and contribute. People feel comfortable asking questions, sharing information informally, and working together to solve problems, creating a culture where people can thrive. Be warned, this only happens when there is no fear that they will be unduly judged or criticised for having new ideas. In low-trust organisations where this is the norm, why would you ever want to put your head above the parapet to be shot at?

Becoming a Cultural Leader

If the quality of teachers' subject knowledge, pedagogy, and classroom teaching is so dependent on a school's culture, then it's dependent on the school leaders to do everything they can to create an environment that supports teachers to improve their teaching.

Indeed, it should be their number one priority and their moral duty to think about the professional development journey of their staff. So they need to think hard about how they can facilitate this by ensuring the teachers' skills and knowledge are being used in the right way. We should ensure that all teachers have the necessary resources they need and that they are given sufficient time to focus on improving their teaching.

It's paramount that we don't let the small stuff get in the way of achieving this. Of course, it's all too easy for that to happen.

Just take a look at Chapter 3 (primary colours model) of Pendleton and Furnham's book 'Leadership: All You Need to Know' (2012). I think it works really well within a school setting, and you'll gain insight into the multifaceted responsibilities leaders face. These responsibilities can be likened to 'big rocks' that need careful arrangement to achieve true leadership.

Their model categorises leadership functions into three domains, each symbolised by a primary colour (red, blue, or green). The 'Strategic' domain outlines the organisational direction, encompassing strategic planning and organisation. The 'Operational' domain involves implementing systems to fulfil the strategic vision. Meanwhile, the 'Interpersonal' domain emphasises relationship-building and talent development, essential components for organisational vitality.

Effective leadership emerges at the intersection of these domains, where rational and emotional elements harmonise. This balance is crucial for resonating with both the intellectual and emotional aspects of the school community.

If you are a school leader who wants to create a positive team culture, then the message is clear: foster a spirit of trust by encouraging all staff to value each other's contributions and care about one another's well-being, and provide them with the opportunity to offer input into how teams within the school work. And the more leaders focus their attention on building effective relationships with teachers, the greater their likely influence on student outcomes. This means you need to get heavily involved in this process by offering your expertise and guidance where you can. Creating a positive team climate will pay dividends, especially during periods of disruption, as we saw with the pandemic.

Effective leadership emerges at the intersection of these domains, where rational and emotional elements harmonise. This balance is crucial for resonating with both the intellectual and emotional aspects of the school community. As Stephen Covey, author of 'The 7 Habits of Highly Effective People,' often described, 'Trust is the glue of life. It's the most essential ingredient in effective communication. It's the foundational principle that holds all relationships.'

There is an essential component to this, without which a culture of trust cannot happen. There needs to be what's known as a sense of psychological safety. I've been talking about this a lot lately, drawing inspiration from Simon Sinek's book 'Leaders Eat Last' (2014). It teaches us the importance of creating a protective circle of safety within our organisations, where everyone feels looked after. It's a lesson I've fully embraced.

Recent research by McKinsey & Company published in De Smet et al. (2021) reveals that a positive team climate has a stronger effect on psychological safety in teams that experienced a greater degree of change in working remotely than in those that experienced less change during the COVID pandemic.

Yet just 43% of all respondents report a positive climate within their team. So a positive team climate is the most important driver of psychological safety and most likely occurs when leaders demonstrate supportive, consultative behaviour that then begins to challenge their teams.

Professional Environments Matter!

Research conducted by Kraft and Papay (2014) shows that teachers typically tend to improve less after 3-4 years of teaching and plateau (see Figure 2.2a). In comparison to Figure 2.3, this evidence would suggest that not all environments are geared to supporting our teachers to continue to grow throughout their careers. How well does your environment work to ensure that teachers, no matter how long they have been teaching, continue to grow?

Teachers with a few years of experience may have formed habits that may not lead to the most desirable results for their students.

Such teachers may also be staying in their performance zone (Eduardo Briceño, 2016). For those of you not familiar with the work of Eduardo Briceño, I highly recommend that you take a look at this, as this is a useful reminder of why many professionals stay in their performance zone rather than the learning zone and become focused-orientated. Here's a great TED Talk from Briceño: 'How to get better at the things you care about' (2016). This is a great summary of what you can do for anyone looking at ways to encourage their teams to move away from their performance zone.

Looking at Figure 2.2b from Kraft and Papay's paper, the dashed line is for teachers who work in the top 25% of schools in terms of professional culture. For example, teachers working in environments where school leaders make adequate time for professional development, student behaviour is excellent, there is an effective performance management system, and teachers collaborate with one another to continue to get better.

The dotted line is for those teachers in schools in the bottom 25% of professional culture. For example, for teachers who are given little guidance from leaders, professional development is not a priority, behaviour is poor, the performance management system is ineffective, and little or no collaboration takes place.

After a decade, teachers in schools ranked at the 75th percentile for professional environment ratings demonstrated a 38% greater improvement than teachers at the 25th percentile, as per Kraft and Papay's findings (2015). This graph suggests that if you work in a school with a rich professional culture, you will have a better chance of continuing to get better and better as a teacher – the quality of teaching matters to student attainment.

I strongly believe that professional environments serve as the backbone for teachers' improvement in our schools and influence their attitudes towards professional development. All the research available to us clearly shows this, and I don't think it's hard to achieve. Tiny adjustments in our school and CPD provision can give us great gains. I'm a strong advocate of this and always offer practical suggestions to create 'thinking environments' in schools, which often costs us no money. I'm delving more into this in Chapter 4.

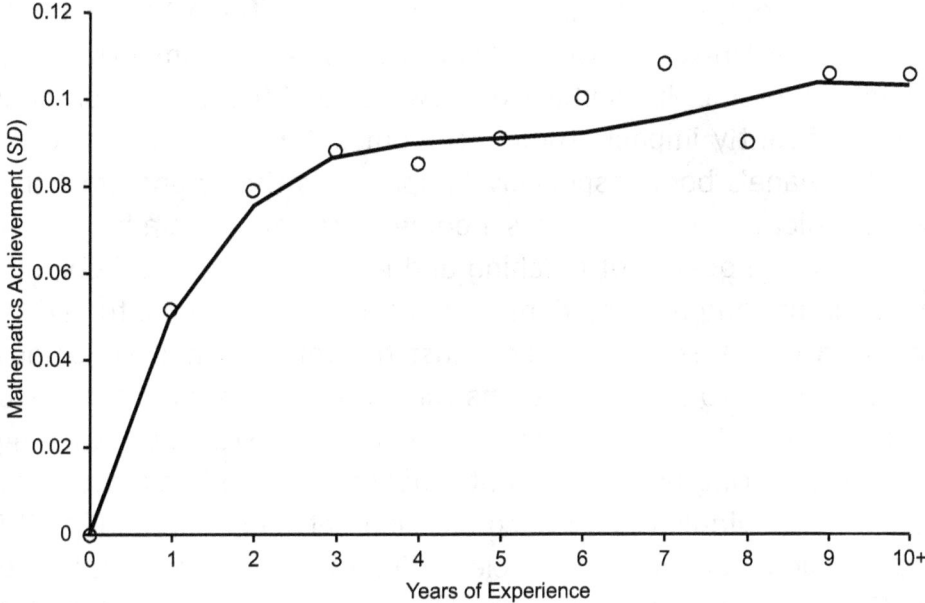

Figure 2.2a Kraft and Papay (2014)

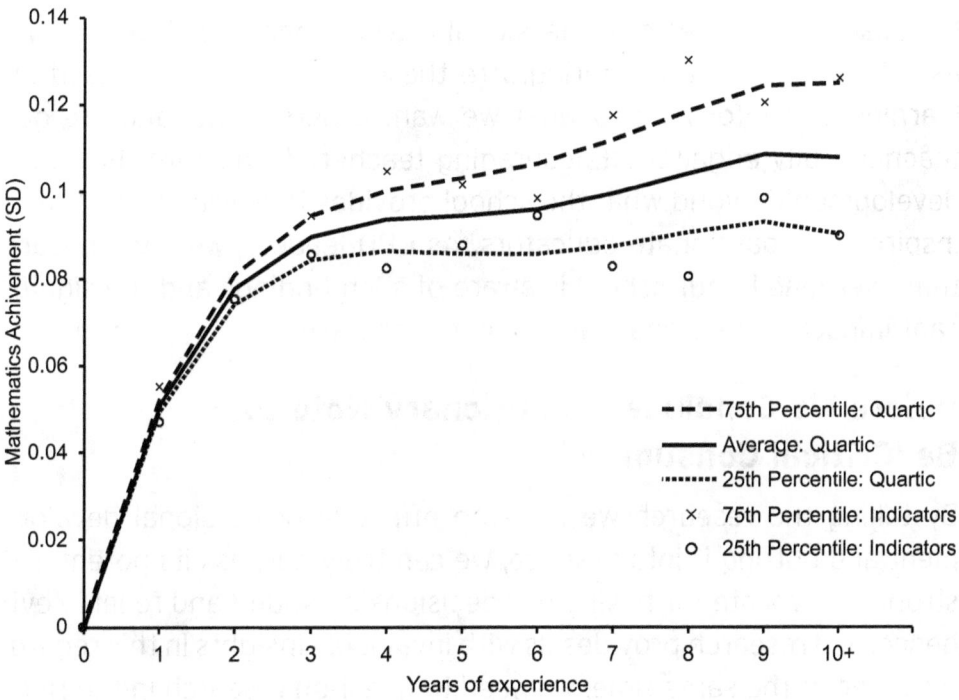

Figure 2.2b Kraft and Papay (2014)

Furthermore, a closer look at the work of Professor Viviane Robinson at the University of Auckland reinforces the importance of school leadership. It emphasises how leaders' focus and approach can significantly impact student outcomes. What I particularly like about Viviane's book, especially Chapter 1, is the strong start that paints a picture showing how school leaders can make a bigger difference in the quality of teaching and learning in their school, ultimately improving their students' performance. According to Viviane Robinson (2011), school leaders must be well-informed about how students learn to identify lessons that will positively influence student learning. One of the five dimensions of student leadership includes ensuring as leaders that teacher learning is a key component, further highlighting the connection between high-quality CPD and excellent teaching. For a clear illustration and explanation of the five dimensions of student leadership, refer to Chapter 1, p. 16 of Viviane's book 'Student-Centered Leadership' (Robinson, 2011).

As school leaders, one of our primary goals should be to promote and actively participate in good professional development. We need to consider the types of professional learning opportunities that we, as school leaders, are offering. Are these opportunities focused on learning or conforming to what we want others to do, and are our teachers fully engaged? Encouraging teachers to nurture their own development beyond what the school provides is crucial for fostering inspired and passionate educators. As CPD leaders, we must ensure that everyone in our school is aware of such findings and the significant impact professional development can have.

Before We Conclude, a Cautionary Note to Be 'Critical Consumers'

By taking the research we have on effective professional development and putting it into practice, we can truly harness its potential. I strongly advocate for basing our decisions on sound and reliable evidence, and research provides us with invaluable insights in this regard. However, at the same time, we need to question research in the right way and judge whether this works in the context we are working in.

I'm slightly concerned that recently, we are losing the importance of this in the UK, and we are becoming faceted on just one or two methods of how we should run our schools. And it is becoming a FAD to talk about research. No one knows and understands better what's needed in a school than the people who are there every day, which is why it is important we invest the time to gain insight into people's ideas and marry this up with some of the strongest research out there. Those of us that are no longer in school full-time have a duty to present a cross-section of the best available research to schools that will help and guide their thinking and decision-making process. This is very important to me. No school leaders or teachers have the time to read all the literature that is out there - even when they say they do. And if we are expecting educators to do this, perhaps this is one of the many reasons we have a recruitment and retention crisis in the UK! It takes me a significant chunk of my week to read all the latest research and updates, so we need to be practical and careful in our approach to how we do this. The more we push in this direction, I fear that this will be another driving factor in pushing colleagues out of the procession.

Pause for Thought!

> How are you using research evidence to guide your decision-making and improve interventions in your school?

With the evidence we have of what makes great teaching, I feel this is very similar to how we should be structuring CPD for teachers. We should offer teachers the same conditions we would give our students: clear goals, tools for successful implementation, scaffolding with lots of practice opportunities, and feedback that guides and informs progress. Unfortunately, many teachers who strive to provide their students with these supports find they are not getting the same in their own professional learning. When designing CPD, we must be aware of this discrepancy and how to get this right. When we are writing a curriculum or scheme of work or planning a lesson, all the ingredients that we know that have the biggest impact on student learning are often similar when we are designing and planning professional development for teachers.

I argue that teachers will perform better when their professional development is catered to their personal needs, they have control over what steps they should take to improve themselves as educators, and enough time is given for them to become familiar and experienced with suitable support and instruction. The results are obvious when these techniques are implemented in our schools: teachers grow and so do student results. Wow, I've just summarised most parts of the book in five sentences! Now that's an achievement!

Conclusion

As we come to the end of Chapter 2, let's take a moment to think about some questions that will enable us to reflect on the importance of teacher quality and why this must never be compromised.

This chapter has made clear the importance of teacher quality and that our role in ensuring this is nurtured and developed should never be compromised. We know that school leaders are the ones who must take responsibility for ensuring that teaching practitioners become even better at what they do.

The challenge, of course, for school leaders is to make sure they are effectively focused on creating not just the practicalities of CPD but also developing the supportive culture that is so necessary for teachers to keep growing. In Chapter 3, we will explore how to make CPD a success and avoid common pitfalls. It's not all doom and gloom, I promise. In the meantime, I'll leave you with these reflection questions to explore and share with your colleagues.

Reflective Questions

1. The quality of teachers we have is paramount, as it has the highest impact on student outcomes. How do you ensure that this remains the driving force behind everything you do in your school?
2. What are you doing to help teachers improve their classroom practice? What's working well, and what needs developing further?
3. How do you celebrate excellent teaching in your school? How can you make this evident across your school community?

4. What is the professional learning culture like in your school? Are your staff members properly included in the development of what's needed?
5. To be the best they can be, staff need to learn from one another. How are you helping them to do this?
6. How do you encourage staff to step outside their comfort zone? Do you know what stops people from stepping outside their comfort zone, and what are you doing to address this issue?
7. How do we ensure that the professional environment for staff is supported with sufficient time for high-quality dialogue and collaboration?
8. To what extent do you ensure that the professional environment in your school not only supports teachers' development but also maintains accountability?
9. How can you build a culture that enables everyone to be in their learning 'sweet spot'?
10. How do you integrate research into your decision-making process at school? How do you critically evaluate and utilise research findings?

Chapter Snapshots

- The quality of teachers we have is paramount, given its significant impact on student outcomes. We ensure that this remains the driving force behind everything we do in our school.
- Expert teachers are those who know how to present and teach subject material using the most appropriate pedagogical methods, develop excellent relationships with their students, and continuously improve their own classroom practice.
- Effective continuous professional development (CPD) is critical to improving the quality of teacher instruction.
- The decline in student attainment during the COVID pandemic, especially among disadvantaged groups and younger learners, highlights the importance of improving teacher skills.

- Change is necessary to improve teacher quality, and strong school leaders must create an environment that embraces change.
- Giving teachers the time to 'sharpen the sword' by allowing them to step back from their classroom commitments and giving them the structured time they need with more expert practitioners to problem-solve and talk about their teaching and pedagogy.
- The right culture creates the conditions that enable everyone to flourish, grow, and become better at what they do.
- Professional environments really matter and make a difference in how teachers improve over time. Peer learning, involving dialogue, lesson observations, and solution-focused thinking are vital for professional growth.
- To create a positive team culture, school leaders should foster a spirit of trust by encouraging all staff to value each other's contributions and care about one another's well-being and provide them with the opportunity to offer input into how teams work within the school.
- We need to integrate research into our school decision-making process; however, at the same time, we need to do this with thoughtful and critical evaluation. This approach will help us inform our strategies effectively and decide what will be most relevant to our school context, giving us the best outcomes for our students.

References

Barber, M. and Mourshed, M. (2007) *How the world's best-performing school systems come out on top.* McKinsey & Company. Available at: https://www.mckinsey.com/~/media/mckinsey/industries/public%20and%20social%20sector/our%20insights/how%20the%20worlds%20best%20performing%20school%20systems%20come%20out%20on%20top/how_the_world_s_best-performing_school_systems_come_out_on_top.pdf.

Briceño, E. (2016) 'Eduardo Briceño: How to get better at the things you care about | TED Talk', *TEDxManhattanBeach*, Manhattan Beach, November.

Available at: https://www.ted.com/talks/eduardo_briceno_how_to_get_better_at_the_things_you_care_about.

Covey, S.M.R. (2020) *The 7 habits of highly effective people*. Revised and updated edition. London: Simon & Schuster UK Ltd.

Covey, S.M.R. and Merrill, R.R. (2008) *The speed of trust: The one thing that changes everything*. New York: Free Press.

De Smet, A. et al. (2021) *Psychological safety and the critical role of leadership development*. Available at: https://www.mckinsey.com/~/media/McKinsey/Business%20Functions/Organization/Our%20Insights/Psychological%20safety%20and%20the%20critical%20role%20of%20leadership%20development/Psychological-safety-and-the-critical-role-of-leadership-development-final.pdf.

Education Endowment Foundation (2022) *The impact of COVID-19 on learning: A review of the evidence*. London: Education Endowment Foundation. Available at: https://d2tic4wvo1iusb.cloudfront.net/documents/guidance-for-teachers/covid-19/Impact_of_Covid_on_Learning.pdf?v=1652815530.

Foer, J. (2012) *Moonwalking with Einstein: The art and science of remembering everything*. 1st edition. London: Penguin.

Hattie, J. (2008) *Visible learning: A synthesis of over 800 meta-analyses relating to achievement*. London: Routledge.

Jeffers, S. (2007) *Feel the fear and do it anyway: How to turn your fear and indecision into confidence and action*. Revised edition. London: Vermilion.

Kraft, M.A. and Papay, J.P. (2014) 'Can professional environments in schools promote teacher development? Explaining heterogeneity in returns to teaching experience', *EducationalEffectiveness and Policy Analysis*, 36(4), pp. 476–500.

Pendleton, D. and Furnham, A. (2012) 'The primary colors of leadership', in D. Pendleton and A. Furnham (eds) *Leadership: All you need to know*. London, UK: Palgrave Macmillan, pp. 45–60. Available at: https://www.researchgate.net/publication/305749027_The_Primary_Colours_of_Leadership.

Pfeffer, J. and Sutton, R.I. (2000) *The knowing-doing gap: How smart companies turn knowledge into action*. Boston, MA: Harvard Business School Press.

Rivkin, S.G., Hanushek, E.A. and Kain, J.F. (2005) 'Teachers, schools, and academic achievement', *Econometrica*, 73(2), pp. 417–458. Available at:

https://hanushek.stanford.edu/sites/default/files/publications/Rivkin%2BHanushek%2BKain%202005%20Ecta%2073%282%29.pdf.

Robinson, V.M. (2011) *Student-centered leadership*. Hoboken: John Wiley & Sons (Jossey-Bass Leadership Library in Education).

Sinek, S. (2014) *Leaders eat last: Why some teams pull together and other don't*. London: Portfolio.

3 Ensuring CPD Is Effective and Avoiding Common Pitfalls

We all have examples of professional development courses we've attended that have had a profound impact on our teaching practice and inspired us to do things differently. Equally, we have all endured training sessions where we have questioned either the expertise of the trainer or the purpose of why we have to do this. The former experience shouldn't be a lottery. Our teachers deserve better. Teacher effectiveness is a key driver for raising student achievement. Your teachers' professional development is one of the most cost-effective interventions that school leaders can put in place. In the UK, on average, teachers spend up to 10.5 days per year attending courses, workshops, seminars, and conferences (Sellen, 2016). Many of the international schools I also work with follow a similar model. We spend a lot of time and money on professional development. Getting professional development right in our schools is imperative.

This chapter will help you to explore the following areas:

- Review the research available on effective teacher continuing professional development (CPD).
- Identify why teacher CPD isn't always as effective as it can be.
- Offer suggestions to be considered by CPD leaders when designing and leading professional development.
- Review the pitfalls and how to avoid them.

The type of high-quality learning experiences that we want from our students, we should also want for (and provide) to teachers.

DOI: 10.4324/9781003232179-3

If we can foster an environment that enables continuous learning, a growth mindset attitude, metacognitive thinking, challenge, and respect in our teachers, then our schools will be world-class institutions. Unfortunately, there are no shortcuts, but the right CPD and robust evaluation of the impact of a CPD programme/s or activity has on classroom practice and student achievement is essential.

Good teaching is not a mystical gift bestowed upon people at birth. It takes time, hard work, continuous reflection, and repeated practice to hone this art. Everyone has the ability to improve, and this belief must be part of the culture we embed across schools (think back to the ideas we touched upon in Chapter 2 and how important this is). If school leaders believe in this and invest their time into supporting this process, our teachers will flourish. Our teachers need the ability to step back and be reflective. Even the most experienced teachers are not finished products; even a master teacher can learn to be even better, which is why CPD is so important.

A concern to ponder is that despite the evidence available to demonstrate that high-quality professional development will improve learning outcomes, improve teacher quality, and make our schools highly effective places to work and learn, schools still continue to play potluck with the quality of their professional development. In 2018, just 38% of teachers felt that professional development resources and time were used in ways that enhanced their practice (Collin and Smith, 2021). Sadly, when CPD is not well-thought-through, rushed, or the lack of support is absent, in most cases, staff will lose interest; they will no longer feel engaged and motivated. When this happens, their professional development will not improve their teaching.

As you read through the next section of this chapter, think about how your current CPD model fits with the current research and the foundations you have in place:

a) supporting key post-holders with responsibility for staff development to be the best they can be
b) supporting teachers to flourish and grow

c) how your CPD provisions are in line with your school improvement plans
d) How do you know this is working?

Effective Professional Development (PD)

High-quality teaching improves student outcomes, and we know that effective teacher PD is a crucial tool to develop teacher quality and enhance student outcomes in the classroom (Hargreaves, 1994; Craft, 2000; Cordingley et al., 2015). High-achieving schools invest heavily in the learning and professional development of their teachers. We need teachers to have excellent subject and pedagogical knowledge. Effective professional development is the key tool to achieving this. We are now very familiar with the Sutton report in 2014, 'What Makes Great Teaching' (Coe et al., 2014), which provides a very useful framework for what has the strongest evidence of improving student achievement. 'Developing Teachers' (The Sutton Trust, 2015) followed in 2015 and provided leaders with some very useful guidance on how we can improve professional development for teachers. What I love about both these reports is the volume of research reviewed to obtain the strongest evidence for what can work. Also, looking through the eyes of a school leader, I appreciate how easily they can be applied to any school context and setting. Both reports make clear that professional development is more likely to be successful when the aims and objectives are aligned with the school improvement plan and there is strong support from the leadership team.

Pause for Thought
- Have you read the earlier reports?
- How well aligned are your professional development objectives to your school improvement plan?
- How well do your leadership team support staff in their progress to-wards both meeting these objectives and knowing why they are necessary?
- Without the ability to measure the positive impact that any training you have provided has had, is it even worthy of the title of 'development'?

How Do We Do This?

1. Develop a Strong Vision

But why?

Start with the 'why,' as simple as it sounds from the words of Simon Sinek (2011) (his work had had such an enormous impact on my leadership development and my everyday practice). I would always start by reflecting on **why** the PD is needed. What do you *need* to achieve both in the short-term and long-term? The fact that you would like your staff to invest their time and energy, while also spending money from your school budget, emphasises the need to carefully consider why this is essential and why we cannot afford to neglect it. Light a fire under your team by creating a reason they all want to get behind.

As well as being very clear on your why, you should also consider how this will fit into the school's improvement priorities. You should also be clear on the investment required (monetary and time) from senior and middle leaders to ensure this is achieved. Considering this will support the starting point to a clear vision.

Having a clear vision is essential to help keep focus. If you know what you are aiming to achieve, you know why this is important, and you know the investment that is being made to get you there, then you will have a focus for your team efforts to get there.

Decide what you are hoping to achieve and work backwards from this. Bear in mind how you will identify the success criteria and which sources you are going to use as evidence to measure the impact of the programme – for example, teacher feedback forms, classroom observations, student data, and feedback from parents. I'll talk more about this in Chapter 7. However, we know that end-of-training questionnaires do not always give us an accurate reflection of how successful a PD activity may be.

Here's an example of a template I often use with schools to '**brain dump**' (a word I love so much right now) our ideas when developing the rationale for a CPD training programme. This template includes the steps we will take to ensure the training is successfully integrated and the methods for assessing its effectiveness. This activity can be as simple or as detailed as you prefer. Still, it enhances the clarity

CPD Rationale	Intended Short-Term CPD Objectives	Intended Long-Term CPD Objectives	Steps for Successful Implementation	Evidence of Impact	Timeline	Leadership Responsibility

of professional development initiatives and addresses both the 'why' and 'how' of the training. Feel free to try it, make improvements, and use it as you see fit, as I often suggest.

2. Duration

Most effective CPD programmes that have lasting impact run over one term, a year, or longer. It is important when designing CPD that consideration is given to how long the programme will run. When working with schools over two or three days, one of my first questions to CPD leads and headteachers is how the work we are going to do will fit in with what you are already doing. What are your long-term CPD objectives, and how can we help you achieve this? Shorter CPD INSETs, twilights, and seminars must be built into the CPD strategic plan for the year so that the vision is not blurred or gets lost along the way. When this doesn't happen, we often get training that makes no sense to staff; they lose interest and will not be able to implement any of the content.

- How much of your current PD takes place over two or three terms?
- How do you connect PD INSETs/twilights/seminars over the term?
- How do you make staff available for your short-/long-term objectives, and what will be achieved at each stage?

3. Manage and Organise

This is crucial. Effective management of the CPD will enable you to ensure that professional development in your school is valued, taken seriously, and successful. As was mentioned in Chapter 2, build a culture where teacher learning is embraced by all regardless of their position or the years of experience they may have. Get the right people on the bus with you and in the correct seats. When designing the CPD programme, consider how you are developing the leadership of others and how you will showcase their talents and hard work across the school or your trust. This is a fantastic opportunity to keep people motivated and to celebrate your successes along the way. The little and often approach is critical to boosting staff morale and showing how far you have come.

Decide from the onset what resources and materials are needed for each CPD activity and programme to be as successful as it possibly can be. And although this may organically lead to new avenues along the way, I always feel that it is an important exercise to undertake with your senior team or those leading the professional development. For example, here, I would identify who will work alongside each other, how often this will happen, and where and when. Leaders who are involved in this process rather than just at the peripheral surface also have a high chance of this benign success, as they will be able to work with their colleagues along the way, sharing their expertise.

- Have a clear CPD calendar that explains when and what will happen over the academic year.
- Identify the expectations of all those involved.
- Check if you have the right resources in place to support implementation (e.g. mentoring or coaching sessions, cycle for peer observations with SLT support).

4. Collaborative Support and Peer Learning

When designing CPD, consider how your colleagues will work together from across your school and subject areas. CPD activities should not just involve reading or listening to subject experts or more experienced practitioners. Teachers should be spending a considerable amount of time practising classroom strategies and not just listening to them. Experiential learning is critical to anyone looking to develop their expertise, so when designing professional development, it is imperative that we move away from a didactic model that simply involves teachers being passive learners. Peer learning amongst professionals is so important to set up, and CPD activities should involve allocated time for purposeful dialogue, low-stake lesson observations and feedback, critical thinking, and solution-focused thinking. There is some excellent evidence of the strong impact that designing teaching and learning communities have on improving teaching. Over the past two years, we've extended our work of establishing teaching and learning communities with our member schools, and the schools have seen some fantastic results as a result of this. Not only has this improved teaching and learning and student achievement but staff are also keen to be involved, as they are seeking the benefits of their work. If you would like further ideas on how to create a Teaching and Learning Community in your school, take a quick read of case study A in Appendix 1 page 185, as well as refer to Chapter 7 of Dylan William's book 'Leadership for Teaching and Learning - Creating a Culture Where All Teachers Improve so That All Students Succeed' (2016).

- How often will your teachers meet to collaborate with their peers?
- How will you overcome some of the barriers to teachers meeting to discuss teaching and learning?
- Do you know enough about teaching and learning communities, and is this feasible in your school right now?

5. Evidence of the Impact on Student Achievement

The primary objective of any professional development programme provided to teachers is to equip them with fresh knowledge and skills that they can utilise to enhance their support for students within the classroom setting. To ensure the effectiveness and impact of such training, it is crucial to align it with student achievement. Therefore, carefully aligning student achievement when designing CPD is the only way we can know and account for whether the training has been successful and impactful. This should be identified and documented in the design stage. For instance, one way to gauge the impact is by tracking changes in student achievement. For example:

- Student achievement increases for a particular group of students

from x to x. Boys' literacy at KS1, for example.
- Half-termly book looks by teachers to review can be valuable in monitoring students' progress throughout the term.
- Gathering direct feedback from students about their learning experiences can provide valuable insights into the effectiveness of the training.

Approaching it from this angle allows us to comprehensively understand the training's impact on both teachers and students.

These five suggestions are quite effective for me and can significantly impact how we think, design, and implement CPD in our schools. Another valuable resource that provides us with plenty of food for thought comes from the EEF, which I'm sure many of you are familiar with. Here's a brief overview:

What Makes Effective Professional Development: EEF Guidance, 2021

The recently published a guidance report on effective PD listing 14 mechanisms that schools and CPD providers should consider when designing and implementing CPD so that it has positive outcomes and is a worthwhile investment. At Veema, we refer to these 14 mechanisms a lot, as they are a helpful framework to us as a CPD provider to ensure that we are designing, implementing, and evaluating the training and school improvement programmes in the most effective way. Figure 3.1 provides an overview of the 14 mechanisms outlined in the report. These 14 mechanisms are split into four groups, which include building knowledge, motivating teachers, developing teaching techniques, and embedding practices. Essentially, the more of these 14 components there are in a professional development programme, the higher the chance there is for this to be successful. Drawing on this framework, you can begin to understand the key ingredients needed for designing professional development activities, which go beyond us looking at just the content. Considering how we present the material and the support we provide pre-, during, and post-training are vital steps to ensuring this will be successful and seen in the classroom.

Ensuring CPD Is Effective and Avoiding Common Pitfalls

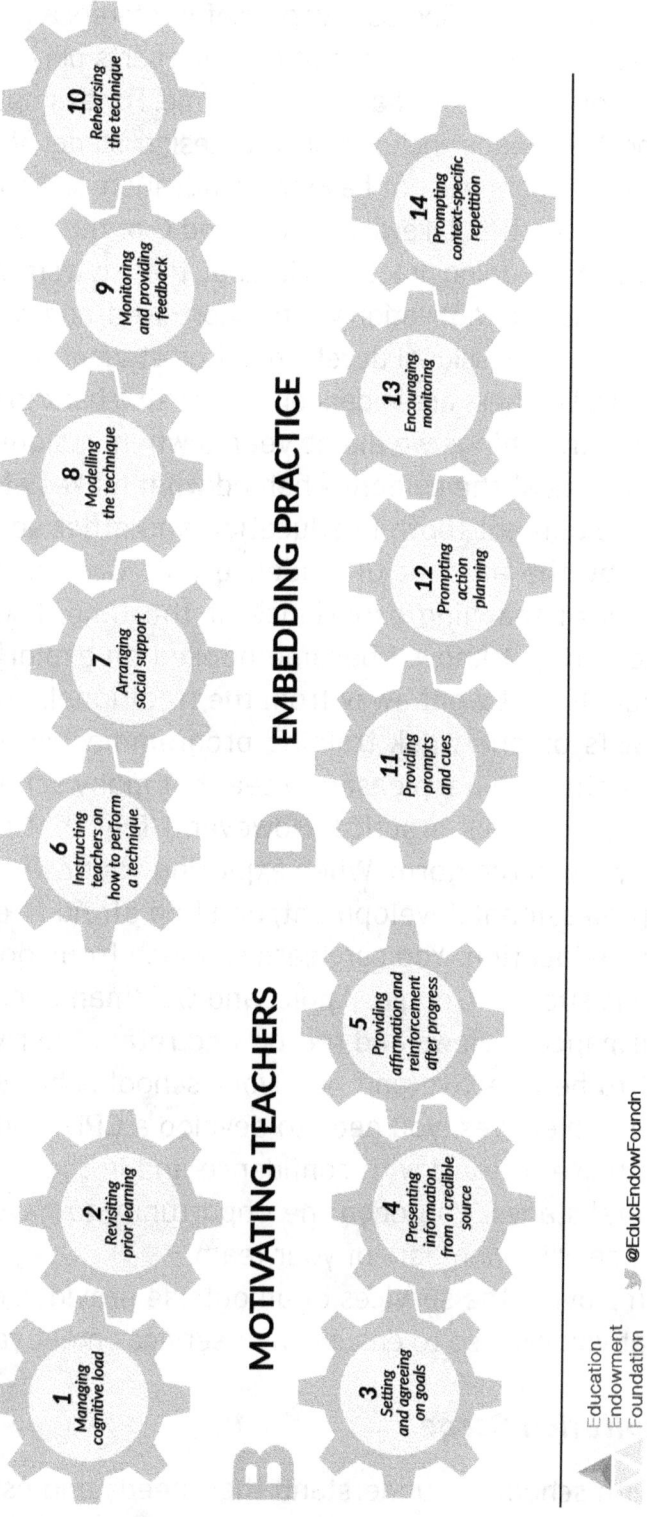

Figure 3.1 Effective Professional Development, Page 29, EEF Guidance Report, October 2021

Furthermore, what I also find as a very useful reference point with the earlier 14 mechanisms is how each of the four parts play a critical role in shaping the effectiveness of a PD programme. For example, if we only have building knowledge included in the design stage of a CPD programme, then teachers will not have the motivation, skills, and support to develop their practice. Likewise, if A, B, and C of the aforementioned are present but embedding practice is left out, there is a strong likelihood that the new skills and motivation will be short-lived, and we will not see the impact of the professional development on student achievement. In such a scenario, teachers are in danger of reverting back to old habits.

One of the first things we did at Veema when designing our CPD model was to look at the evidence behind what makes effective professional development (both in education and other sectors). I was blown away by the amount of evidence that was out there. With over 18 years of teaching experience at the time, I was shocked at how much I didn't know. I became hooked on exploring alternative CPD models that went away from the traditional, less effective, one-off INSETs or one-week training programmes we used to see delivered in schools. I am pleased to see that many schools are now moving away from this practice. However, I feel that in 2013, this was still very much the norm. When exploring your own approach to designing professional development, don't be afraid to explore avenues beyond education. You can learn so much from looking at how organisations such as Google, Apple, and Goldman Sachs structure their performance reviews and recruit and retain their workforce.

For CPD to be effective and help your school achieve the school improvement objectives, you need to develop a CPD model that enables you to move forward with confidence and in the right direction in incremental stages. You need the opportunity to have structured reflection time with members of your team.

When employing the services of an outside provider, consider the process that you will use to ensure their services meet your needs.

The Consultation Stage

We meet with schools to understand their needs and establish what they are hoping to achieve to identify the vision, aims, objectives, audience, and timeframe. The consultation stage is imperative to determine whether everyone has the same vision for the outcomes of the work. The whole team, both external and internal, should know the specific and measurable outcomes that we are all moving towards. Quite often, this may involve two or three school visits and redrafting of CPD proposals. The time spent on outlining details together is necessary to get it right.

Having a clear vision and knowing we are going to celebrate and identify success points and the impact of our work are part of tailoring a personalised approach to CPD.

At This Stage, We Tend to Do the Following:

- Collate information and ask lots of questions.
- Dive deep to discover our current position and identify the desired goals.
- Emphasise why the CPD is necessary and assess whether we are right for you!

The Tailoring Stage

In the next stage, we work together to design a bespoke CPD programme that meets the needs identified in the consultation stage. This is where the bespoke training package comes to life. It should be unique to your school.

No school context is the same, and although we have a good understanding of some great things that work in improving our schools and classroom teaching, we must adapt our approach to ensure that we are meeting the needs of different school contexts and cultures. This is particularly important to us at Veema since many of the projects we are assigned involve working with international schools, where their starting point and what is considered statutory training or legislation in their country are very different from the UK.

At This Stage, We Tend to Do the Following:

- We create a bespoke training programme with clear aims, objectives, and timelines.

- We collaborate with key stakeholders to ensure their input is coherent throughout.
- We personalise and clarify that our work can organically evolve over 6-18 months.

The Training Stage

This is where the nuts and bolts of the earlier stages come to life. The training sessions begin and involve a variety of formats: seminars, one-to-one coaching, in-class team teaching, peer observation, setting up and leading teaching and learning communities and instructional coaching. This is where the magic really happens, and our work gets off the ground.

At this stage, leaders can often sit back and let outside consultants take over. However, it is crucial for leaders to remember the bigger picture outlined in the consultation stage. Are we achieving our vision? How is this leading us towards our goals? How am I monitoring the impact of the training? All of this should be planned during the consultation stage. A great leader will remain focused at every stage of this journey.

At This Stage, We Tend to Do the Following:

- Training is delivered in various formats, whether from the front or through team teaching and modelling.
- Teachers and school leaders initiate the process of acquiring new knowledge and skills and are encouraged to be reflective and problem-solvers.
- Adjustments are made to tailor the training to the specific context

The Reflection Stage

Veema's aim was to be different from other providers. The key component of our CPD model is to make sure that time is given for teachers and leaders to be reflective on their learning process. We plan opportunities for stakeholders to work with others collaboratively and refine key areas they have been working on during the training. Participants should be able to identify specifically what they are going to do next. Reflective practice is encouraged throughout the whole process, from consultation to the final reflection.

The final reflection stage of our CPD model is vital for the implementation of new skills and facilitates long-term change with our support. During this phase, we can look back upon successes. We can explore issues and make plans for the next steps. Although this phase is named 'final reflection,' this is not the end. It is the beginning of the next phase for the school. All lessons learned are reviewed in order to make the right next steps for the school.

At This Stage, We Tend to Do the Following:

- Encourage the reflective practice that has been ongoing since the beginning to be systematically reviewed and departmentalised with concrete steps.
- Assess whether the aims and objectives have been achieved.
- Celebrate successes, refine processes as needed, and identify areas for potential change.

I hope the areas I've addressed so far are relevant to you when thinking and planning your CPD activities, drawing from some of my own experiences. Now, I would like to draw attention to some areas I feel we should try to avoid. I've humorously labelled these as the 'six deadly' errors.

Six Deadly Errors to Avoid When Planning Your Professional Development

Error 1: Taking a Top-Down Approach to CPD

Consider this: Include all stakeholders and staff in the design process of the professional development. This will not only increase your chance of buy-in and trust from your colleagues but it will also enable you to cater for individual needs. This chapter has shown just how important it is for staff to feel a part of their professional development journey.

Error 2: Didactic CPD – Just Tell Them, and They'll Know How to Do It

You can tell teachers how to do things as much as you like. This won't change anything. Unless practitioners explore ideas and concepts in their own time and work on manageable bite-size chunks to get better at a particular area of their teaching practice, little will change.

Consider this: Give teachers the information they need and the evidence behind it but allow them to structure their own way of practising this. When designing your CPD, make sure that you model what you are looking for but also facilitate the time for teachers to work together to develop their own strategies that will work best for them. Do not hope that they will then practise without support. Instead, include clear action points that are agreed upon by everyone. Set deadlines for reflecting back, and allow them to share their experience from their own classroom. This approach of collaborative reflection will support positive habit formation. Teachers will get used to exploring what works for them and what does not work and will build the habit of reflective practice because of your inclusive process.

Error 3: Running INSETs and Twilights Without Planning Any Follow-Up

Stand-alone training events and any external consultant/trainers working with the school will only be productive and value for money if a clear follow-up plan is developed. Staff should know how they will work together following any whole-school INSETs and twilights to make an impact on student outcomes. Many schools are doing fantastic work in this area, but I always feel we can get better at how we approach this. We could better align CPD so that they follow on from each other as well as reflect back on things we have already covered to enhance our knowledge and expertise.

Consider this: When planning your whole-school training in consultation with your staff, make sure you include and list follow-up activities that teachers will participate in. Make the time used as valuable as it can be by providing the path everyone will follow. In Appendix 1,

I have provided a CPD template you may wish to use to help you plan your follow-up activities to your whole-school training events. This has been adapted from Gibbs' six-step reflective cycle (Gibbs, 1988). I would recommend here that you refer to the areas I have addressed in this chapter, in particular, the guidance given by the EEF on effective professional development.

Error 4: Only Allowing Time for Professional Development at the Start and End of Term

As we know, outstanding schools make time for teachers to develop and craft their teaching practices. This is an opportunity for you to think more creatively in how you plan, design, and implement CPD opportunities for your staff.

Consider this: Structure time across the academic year that is specifically allocated to professional development that **all** staff follow. With an emphasis on **all staff** here. This should be done at least once a fortnight or even weekly to enable practitioners to come together. You may wish to consider having a layered approach to CPD that includes the following:

- Week 1: All staff meet to come together for whole-school-focused CPD
- Week 2: Departmental time and subject-specific CPD
- Week 3: Professional development workshops, speeches on individual learning time
- Week 4: Coaching meetings and teaching learning communities meet

Error 5: Not Evaluating Your CPD

More on this will follow in Chapter 7. However, I'd like to take this opportunity to mention this briefly here. This is an area of CPD that largely gets ignored. If we don't evaluate the quality of a CPD programme, then we won't know how useful it has been. We won't know its impact on improving teaching and learning or (most importantly) student achievement.

Consider this: As well as teacher feedback surveys, try to include other forms of evidence to measure the impact of your professional development. This should be considered in the early planning stages.

You could plan to use the following:

- low-stakes lesson observations
- teacher interviews
- evidence from student assessments
- evidence from student exercise books
- student voice surveys
- parental voice surveys

Whatever you choose to use, plan during the early stages. All stakeholders should clearly know what they hope to see if the implementation is going successfully. That way, you will know what you are looking for as you gather your evidence.

Error 6: Failure to Integrate Online CPD With In-Person Training

Online training has been great, and for many of us, this was a large part of our CPD during COVID. However, the mistake that we see many schools making with this service is that this is very rarely followed up with staff. We may get a certificate of participation at the end of an online training session. How can we be sure that the knowledge and level of understanding we need on a particular area has really been understood by staff? Without the opportunity for teachers to revisit this material, this will soon become a tick-box exercise that we simply ask staff to do without concern about the outcome.

Consider this: When planning CPD, if you use online platforms for safeguarding child protection, or more specifically, teaching and learning courses, try to embed a half-term mini activity that staff can complete to show you their current knowledge and understanding. Just like with our students, learning gaps after long periods of time are likely. Your planned follow-ups should allow staff time to reflect upon the course they have taken and any learning gaps that may have occurred over the passage of time. It might be that follow-up training is needed, or it might be that they just needed the opportunity to refresh their learning by revisiting the material. You can do this by creating a short online quiz and conversation starter questions to be discussed in departmental meetings or briefings with answers recorded.

Conclusion

In this chapter, we have explored what constitutes effective CPD for teachers and examined the available evidence on how to approach the planning and implementation of professional development in our schools. We have also discussed what to avoid and highlighted essential practices. We recognise that CPD plays a crucial role in enhancing teaching skills and fostering improvement. However, poorly executed CPD can hinder teacher development. The strongest evidence has been presented to assist you in considering your own needs when designing effective teacher CPD. While time constraints may introduce skepticism about practical implementation, Chapter 4 will delve into how we can manage our time for quality CPD in our schools, change mindsets and habits, and support teacher development.

Reflective Questions

1. As a practitioner, what makes good CPD?
2. How do you support those who lead teacher development in your school?
3. Over the past two years, what changes have you made to your CPD model?
4. How will you use the 2021 guidance report produced by the EEF to inform your school's CPD model?
5. How do we ensure that professional development time is used productively and that all colleagues perceive the relevance of their work?
6. What aspects do you avoid when planning CPD in your school? Are they similar to the areas addressed in this chapter?
7. What follow-up activities do you plan after whole-school CPD, and how are they communicated to teachers?

8. How do we meet the needs of individuals at the same time as meeting the needs of the school as a whole?
9. How do we measure the impact of our work?
10. How could establishing a teacher learning community (TLC) across your school contribute to the improvement of teachers' classroom practices and facilitate collaborative learning experiences?

Chapter Snapshots

1. Teachers in the UK invest an average of up to 10.5 days per year in professional development.
2. Effective teaching requires continuous effort, reflection, and practice, emphasising that improvement is achievable for all educators.
3. In 2018, just 38% of teachers believed professional development resources and time improved their teaching practice.
4. High-quality teaching significantly impacts student outcomes, making effective teacher professional development essential.
5. Having a clear vision of what you hope to achieve for the professional development activity is crucial alongside why the CPD is taking place, the short-term and long-term goals, and a plan for how the new learning and skills will be implemented as well as supported to make adjustments are vital.
6. Consideration of programme duration is essential, as most impactful professional development programmes run over one term, a year, or longer.
7. The EEF's 14 mechanisms for effective professional development are grouped into four categories, including knowledge building, motivation, teaching techniques, and practice embedding. Including as many of these mechanisms in a CPD activity or programme increases the likelihood of successful professional development.
8. The six deadly errors in planning CPD include the following: taking a top-down approach, relying on didactic methods, conducting INSETs and twilights without follow-up planning, limiting professional development time to the start and end of term, neglecting CPD evaluation, and failing to integrate online CPD with in-person training.

References

Coe, R., Aloisi, C., Higgins, S. and Major, L.E. (2014) *What makes great teaching? Review of the underpinning research*. London: Sutton Trust. Available at: https://www.suttontrust.com/our-research/great-teaching/

Collin, J. and Smith, E. (2021) *Effective professional development guidance report*. London: Education Endowment Foundation. Available at: https://d2tic4wvo1iusb.cloudfront.net/eef-guidance-reports/effective-professional-development/EEF-Effective-Professional-Development-Guidance-Report.pdf.

Cordingley, P. et al. (2015) *Developing great teaching: Lessons from the international reviews into effective professional development*. London: Teacher Development Trust. Available at: https://tdtrust.org/wp-content/uploads/2015/10/DGT-Full-report.pdf.

Craft, A. (2000) *Continuing professional development: A practical guide for teachers and schools*. London: Routledge.

Gibbs, G. (1988) *Learning by doing: A guide to teaching and learning methods*. Oxford: Oxford Further Education Unit.

Hargreaves, A. (1994) *Changing teachers, changing times: Teachers' work and culture in the postmodern age*. London: Cassell (Teacher Development).

Sellen, P. (2016) *Teacher workload and professional development in England's secondary schools: Insights from TALIS*. Education Policy Institute. Available at: https://dera.ioe.ac.uk/id/eprint/27930/1/TeacherWorkload_EPI.pdf.

Sinek, S. (2011) *Start with why: How great leaders inspire everyone to take action*. New York: Portfolio/Penguin.

The Sutton Trust (2015) *Developing teachers*. London: The Sutton Trust. Available at: https://www.suttontrust.com/our-research/developing-teachers-professional-development-pupil-attainment/.

William, D. (2016) *Leadership for teacher learning: Creating a culture where all teachers improve so that all students succeed*. West Palm Beach, FL: Learning Sciences International.

4 Habits of Great Leaders That Work in Times of Crisis and Give Us Time to Improve

One of the significant reasons CPD initiatives fail is that not enough time is given to either their initial delivery or subsequent evaluation. All too often, we rush in with a 'quick' fix that we hope will work and then expect overnight miracles that never happen. If we are going to improve the quality of our teaching, and consequently, the outcomes for our pupils, then we must build sufficient time to help teachers perfect their craft.

In this chapter, we will do the following:

- Identify strategies for leading with agility, fostering a shift towards doing things differently.
- Focus on cultivating effective habits in our school to support teacher development.
- Explore practical and easy-to-implement ideas for cultivating thinking environments, both within our schools and among our teachers.

We know only too well how pushed for time we are in schools. We have so much to accomplish in a school year that it can often feel overwhelming to leaders. The time we have available (or lack of it) often seems to work against us. In recent years, many new challenges have eaten up our precious time. For example, ensuring school safety during a pandemic. Many of us are working to the point of burnout. When unforeseen crises arise, many initiatives and school priorities are placed at the bottom of the list as we face the unknown.

Leaders had to operate quickly to ensure that online lessons took place, training for teachers was in place, and systems to monitor student attendance and well-being were set up. And all at a time when we had lots of chopping and changing government COVID guidelines: 'Yes, we can' one minute, followed by 'No, we can't' the next, finding out at 6 pm whether the school will reopen the next day or stay online. Headteachers were constantly on call, early 5 am starts, and new policies drawn up daily, redrafted, and then redrafted again and again, with students not having access to laptops or broadband. Headteachers and teachers worked around the clock to provide the very best care to their students, parents, and staff. Often with very little time away from school during the holidays, they made sure plans and systems (as best they could be) were in place for the start of term. It's tiring just reading this back.

If you are new to leadership and did not live through this particular crisis, you can gain an insight into the reality of living through it in this online interview with headteachers:

https://www.youtube.com/watch?v=JGP2BOAFb6Q.

As you read this, I am sure many of you are having sudden flashbacks of everything you did during the coronavirus pandemic. Challenging to say the least! I am also sure that you can recognise many achievements that were made over this time. Everything gets done in the end. It is only when we are out of the panic that we can look back and say that. However, having lived through at least one major crisis, you can use this as food for thought as you plan for the next. When you find yourself saying, 'I don't have time,' remember, all we have is time. It is what you do with that time that counts.

Skills of an Agile Leader

Agile leadership requires a flexible, adaptive approach. It doesn't depend on static strategies but rather, adjusts as needed based on the situation. Agile leaders are able to make smart decisions and generate new ideas. They assess all aspects of a problem before responding and embrace feedback from themselves and their team members. Agile leaders create an environment where employees can thrive, encouraging them to innovate and reach their full capacity.

Agile leaders have specific skills that enable them to effectively lead and manage their time during any crisis. They anticipate needs before they arise, are comfortable with making decisions without complete information, understand how technology can be used to maximise time, and are able to communicate with precision to stakeholders. They take risks (even in uncertain times), create a culture that encourages effective and time-saving collaboration across departments and disciplines, manage stress effectively, and remain flexible as conditions change rapidly.

During times of crisis, having the ability to think strategically about long-term solutions while responding quickly when necessary will save precious time.

Communicating clearly with all stakeholders means everyone is kept up-to-date on changes or new initiatives being implemented at the school level. Clear communication leaves very little room for others to misunderstand and so saves leaders time when they do not have to revisit the communication.

Agile leaders also have empathy for staff members who are struggling during difficult times, while also holding them accountable for their work. In a crisis, we must act fast but, at the same time, with flexibility and understanding while still getting the job done.

Agile leaders know that good habits made visible will support all staff in pulling together when a crisis hits. You may have worked diligently on your three- or five-year improvement plan. However, when the crisis happens, you need everyone to recognise that the priorities have now changed, and you must work together to all do the best for your students. When a crisis hits, time is not on your side. There will always be occasions in school when we have to act quickly.

Pause for Thought – Agile Leadership Quick Reference

Take this as an opportunity to self-assess your agility. Push it a bit further and get two of your colleagues to do the same assessment on you. Then look back at their answers and compare them with your own reflections. This questionnaire can also be found in Appendix 4.

By completing this short reflection exercise, what does it reveal about you? What stops us from becoming agile leaders? The responsibility we bear towards our students, teachers, governors, parents, or school

Table 4.1

	Tick ✓	Give an Example
I provide my staff with an opportunity to participate in school-level decisions.		
I articulate my views to others and seek out feedback before giving a final call.		
I make sure to plan regular times when I and the staff at my school can get together with other educators and teachers so that we can learn from them.		
I make well-thought-out plans, but I'm willing to modify them if need be.		
I give people leeway to make decisions based on their experience and authority.		
I accept responsibility for my missteps and discuss this with my team.		
I'm constantly learning and evolving, developing creative solutions to changing demands.		
I welcome fresh ideas without any hesitations.		
If it's beneficial for students and staff, I'm unafraid to take calculated risks.		
I'm unafraid to take calculated risks.		

owners. Perhaps it's just easier for us to follow the script. However, one thing I have particularly learned through the pandemic and my increased self-reliance in recent years is the importance of developing my agility. For me, adding this essential leadership skill to our toolbox is crucial because our school context can vary greatly, and unexpected events can lead us in different directions. This brings me to the importance of cultivating good habits, which is essential for achieving our objectives. When planning effective professional development, we must offer staff the opportunity to establish good habits and eliminate bad ones.

Forming good habits is not an overnight process. Good school leaders and teachers are those who can be the following:

- Flexible
- Adaptative
- Resilient
- Solution-focused thinking
- Seeing learning through the eyes of their students
- Reflective practitioner
- Problem-solvers
- Empathetic

When deciding upon the habits you want your teachers to have, having a clear strategic direction and a clear vision that is supported by educational research is vital. We must convince external stakeholders such as the chair of governors or school owners, who are often not qualified educators, of the impact that good professional development has on raising school standards. We need such stakeholders to understand that success will not be achieved with just any old training or your good friend from a nearby school comes to deliver some INSET. Professional development needs to be a well-thought process involving all staff.

Professor Robert Coe's (2020) paper 'The Case for Subject-Specific CPD' draws attention to the impact of investing in teacher professional development on student achievement. He outlines five core components:

1. Sustained duration – to be considered continuous, the professional development should be over 15 hours.
2. Content: Focuses on improving teachers' knowledge.
3. Active: Opportunities to try it out and discussions are encouraged, acknowledging that it takes time to get things right.
4. Supported: External feedback is provided, and staff networks are in place for ongoing improvement and sustainability.
5. Evidence-based: Learning walks are conducted to assess the impact of recent CPD or training in the classroom.

The aforementioned are all essential elements of successful continuous teacher education across two terms or more. Of course, there is still a place for the 'sheep-dip' approach; everyone has the same training because of the statutory obligations, e.g. safeguarding and child protection, health and safety and first aid. If we are looking at developing skills and expertise to a mastery level, then we need to consider three things:

1. The systems we create in schools for teachers to build effective teaching habits. And break bad ones!
2. How do we bring others on board and motivate staff to be the best versions of themselves?
3. How do we shrink the change to lead school-wide change that sticks?

Habit Formation and Behaviour Change

You may have heard of the three Rs to building successful habits which include reminders, routines, and rewards. How do you embrace the three Rs to ensure that professional development is of the highest quality in your school? How is your school CPD designed to support staff to develop their habits and expertise, and how do you encourage innovation and creativity and allow people to step outside of their comfort zone for trial and error?

One area I believe schools should prioritise more is understanding the psychology behind habit development. If we can truly understand the psychology behind forming habits and are given the opportunity to explore this, it could greatly enhance professional development. This goes beyond merely covering pedagogical or leadership topics. We need to genuinely recognise and acknowledge (and with this care) the positive impact this has on our professional learning journeys. I am constantly trying to remind myself to include this aspect in my own training and engage in discussions with other school leaders on how to effectively implement it. It's so easy for us to ignore this despite its significance.

To enable people to grow professionally, you need to create opportunities for people to change their habits. David Brailsford revolutionised sports performance when he applied the concept of **marginal gains** to Team GB's cycling programme leading up to the 2004 Olympic Games. His strategy focused on optimising every aspect of preparation – no matter how small it seemed – resulting in a historic medal haul for British athletes. The same approach I believe can be applied to helping teachers improve – laying everything out and making things obvious about what you are going to do.

Developing Teachers Through Purposeful Practice

Deliberate practice has become a common term currently used in education. Recently, the idea of the 10,000 hours needed to achieve mastery has been questioned. A method employed by sports and professional athletes for years, it is now an increasingly popular topic for educators. Although achieving expertise requires hours of hard work, experience alone does not improve performance.

Understanding how to embed deliberate practice can help master techniques, building practice and in-tune learning towards forming good habits and breaking bad ones. Simply put, deliberate practice is the process of focused effort, repetition, feedback, and further refinement to improve a skill. Breaking things down into manageable chunks, deliberate practice requires intense concentration and feedback from a knowledgeable source to maximise improvement. Practising specific teaching techniques, guided by clear criteria defining what 'good' looks like and crafted by an expert practitioner capable of offering focused feedback, is essential for bridging the 'knowing-doing' gap and developing effective habits that develop a technique you are looking to improve.

Although deliberate practice is not the only method for improving teachers, engaging in practice is valuable. It allows teachers to hone their craft by engaging in activities that will help them become more proficient with their teaching methods. The goal of deliberate practice is not simply mastery but continual improvement of skills over time. This can include improving lesson delivery, developing better classroom management strategies, and experimenting with new teaching techniques or any other activity that can help teachers grow professionally, such as handling a difficult conversation with a parent.

Deliberate practice is an effective tool for assisting teachers to improve their teaching practices over time because it builds effective habits.

'Practice with Purpose,' published by Deans for Impact (2016), provides an excellent model of deliberate practice, which includes five fundamental principles to maximise the growth and development of teacher expertise. I've adapted the principles given to us in this report later to help illustrate how we might utilise deliberate practice with teacher CPD. You can find the full report, 'Practice with Purpose: The Emerging Science of Teacher Expertise,' by Deans for Impact at the following link: https://www.deansforimpact.org/files/assets/practice-with-purpose.pdf.

These principles include the following:

- Pushing beyond one's comfort zone
- Working towards specific goals
- Focused practice
- Providing high-quality feedback
- Having an excellent understanding of high-quality teaching

Push Beyond One's Comfort Zone

Push beyond your comfort zone; I've emphasised its importance throughout the book. Being in your challenge sweet spot is crucial. If it's too easy, you aren't cultivating new skills. To develop, we must push beyond our comfort zones. This is a crucial component of effective professional development, making a significant difference. Gaming designers excel at this, designing games for optimum engagement.

Working Towards Specific Goals

Deliberate practice involves working towards specific skills; teachers play a vital role in this process and are not merely subject to decisions made for them. Practice tasks should be very specific, progressing from the easiest to the most difficult. As James Clear mentioned, ensure that goals not only dictate what you do but also have good systems in place for achievement.

Focus Intensively

Deep concentration and purposeful effort from novices are essential for improvement. This includes opportunities to practice in different areas beyond the classroom. How do you achieve this? Through meetings, one-on-one sessions, school visits, and online learning. Strip away impediments hindering your practice.

High-Quality Feedback

Provide feedback promptly after teachers practice specific teaching techniques. Gain expert feedback and use it to correct, stretch, and refocus on areas needing improvement. Feedback should be part of the continuous loop.

Mental Models

Mental models of expertise guide and provide opportunities for reflection and monitoring to improve performance. By having these mental models, we understand what expertise looks like, aiding us on the journey. Teachers should understand how students learn, grasp new ideas, and retain information from cognitive science. This will help them to make adjustments to what you are doing.

Pause for Reflection
- How familiar are you with deliberate practice and the report by Deans for Impact?
- What elements do you find most useful to embed in your CPD programmes?
- How do you ensure that teachers in your school have a clear mental model of what 'good' looks like to benchmark where they are currently at?

The Power of Tiny Habits Over Long Periods of Time

In his book, 'Atomic Habits,' James Clear (2008) teaches readers how to build good habits and break bad ones. Clear states, 'You do not rise to the level of your goals. You fall to the level of your systems.' This means that it is not enough to set a goal simply; it is essential to create a system of good habits that will help you meet your goals. While this may seem obvious, many people don't realise that bad habits can also work against them. If we go back to the work of Kraft and Papay (2017) from Chapter 2, we can see that professional environments really matter, and if we don't provide the opportunity for colleagues to feel challenged to grow and get better, performance decreases.

By helping individuals develop tiny habits that can lead to big changes over time, I feel this book is an invaluable tool for school leaders and teachers who want to make positive changes in their schools. Let's take a look at why 'Atomic Habits' is so effective.

'Atomic Habits' focuses on the power of small changes over time that can lead to lasting effects. Being 1% better each day can eventually lead to massive improvements. By providing teachers with the space for reflection and review of that habit, you can be on to something really good.

By focusing on tiny habits such as going for a 20-minute walk every morning/evening or taking a few minutes each day to stay organised, you can gradually create larger shifts in your life and behaviour. This principle applies to schools too; by focusing on small changes that we'd like teachers to develop, we can create an environment where everyone feels supported and respected. An effective way to change a habit is to focus not on what you want to achieve but on what you wish to become. Whether we choose to accept it or not, people are often products of where they are and not what they are.

The Four Laws of Behaviour Change

'Atomic Habits' by James Clear (2018) has really got me thinking. Firstly, we definitely need to include the art of breaking and forming new habits to any CPD we run and not on a light touch add-on. Secondly, I really like how we should perhaps shift our mindsets from focusing our attention on creating systems for building good habits rather than setting ourselves targets. And I'll come onto this a little more in a moment. Thirdly, the four laws of behaviour change in the book – make it obvious, make it attractive, make it easy, and make it satisfying – are easy to use and make it essential for creating lasting change. In comparison, to break a habit, we must make it invisible, unattractive, difficult, and unsatisfying.

By following these laws when introducing new behaviours or practices into the school setting, school leaders and teachers can ensure that their efforts will be successful. For example, if a teacher wants students to participate more actively in class discussions, they should make it obvious by assigning roles for each student each day, make it attractive by offering incentives for participation, make it easy by providing clear instructions for how to participate, and finally, make it satisfying by giving students positive feedback when they do participate. If we'd like teachers to be talking about teaching and learning and ways they can improve their instruction, we must provide the resources and space for them to do this.

So how do we support teachers to develop good habits based on the advice we have for good teaching whilst breaking bad ones? Here are some ideas, and by all means, this is not an exhaustive list.

Make the Habit Obvious

Give teachers the evidence that supports a teaching approach as well as showing how it looks in practice. Allow them time to experiment and observe the approach in action. Create systems that remind them of the teaching pedagogies they should be using: visuals around the school, bite-size professional development material in the staffroom, and allocated time for staff to meet up and discuss teaching and learning by setting up teaching and learning communities.

Make the Habit Attractive

Motivate staff by praising their efforts on a termly cycle. Recognise everyone for how far they've come, and provide a platform for them to talk about the journey they have taken. Create a blog post, a video, or incentives like teacher exchange programmes, collaborations with other schools, or career progression routes.

Make the Habit Easy to Master

There is no point in asking teachers to try out new things if you are going to make it difficult for them. Giving no time comes to mind here! If we want our teachers to get better and adopt better teaching habits, really work hard to identify what they will do. Make the journey easy. This means planning to the T, scripting everything, and using checklists to ensure everything is in place (e.g. 'Meetings will take place at these dates and time,' 'We will cover xxx,' 'Attendance is compulsory,' 'Follow-up actions are explicit and specific.')

Make the Habit Satisfying

Teachers should enjoy the experience of developing their craft. Working on managing a habit should make someone feel good and give them a sense of accomplishment. Just like our students, they should get the right level of dopamine fixes released in their brains (more on this will follow shortly). Make acquiring the habit fun through teamwork and trying new things.

Similarly, if we want to encourage teachers to stop using a particular teaching style or a pedagogical strategy that does not create positive outcomes for our learners, then we must ensure that we are giving teachers the right information and resources that will eventually stop them from using ineffective teaching techniques and replacing them with effective ones like formative assessment. This is why I feel that coaching and, in particular, instructional coaching work so well for forming great habits. It provides regular support and the time for dialogue to reflect and plan on mastering expertise.

Focus on Habit Stacking

The key to developing effective systems for success is habit stacking. Habit stacking is when you combine several small actions into one larger action or system. For this strategy to be effective, it needs to be broken down into specific steps so that each part can be accomplished easily and quickly. In a classroom setting, this could mean having students start each day by organising their notebooks, writing down the agenda for the day, and reviewing any upcoming assignments or tests before getting started on their work. By teaching students how to stack these small tasks together in an efficient manner, they will develop better organisational skills overall, which can help them stay ahead of their studies and succeed in school.

For habit stacking to be successful, you need to make the habit obvious and attractive, which includes the right conditions for the change to stick. Going too quickly will force people to step back and resist the change. I know in schools, we are faced with many external stakeholders, mainly inspectorates, that add additional pressure to make change happen quickly as time ticks away till the next visit. But it is important to take into account the science behind how successful change happens, and this requires strategic thinking and strong leadership, which is what any inspection team should understand with the evidence and story you provide. Drawing on the work of Chip

Heath and Dan Heath from their book 'Switch – How to Change Things When Change Is Hard' (2011) gives us a clear picture of how we help others change. To change behaviour, we need to direct the rider (the rational part of our human brain, the prefrontal cortex), motivate the elephant (the emotional side, appeal to people's hearts), and shape the path (the environment).

All three of the aforementioned need each other to work. If the rider goes too fast and the destination is not clear, we know what the elephant will do. I'm not sure about you, but GOOD LUCK trying to shift an elephant when it doesn't want to move. One of the main reasons why many CPD and school improvement initiatives do not achieve their desired change is that we've failed to marry the rider with the elephant. We see this all the time, and we have to be honest about how we can get better at supporting better professional practice. In the 23 years I've worked with schools, when we haven't achieved the desired outcomes, it's largely been due to moving too quickly-running at full speed without taking careful, incremental steps-and not making sufficient adjustments to the environment to support behavior change.

Figure 4.1 Behaviour Change: Directing the Rider and Motivating the Elephant

As CPD leaders, how can we implement Chip and Dan's work into planning, structuring, and delivering CPD in our schools? In Table 4.2, I've included some ideas for consideration on how the rider-elephant analogy can be applied to our school context when thinking about effective CPD and building relationships. For me, the book 'Switch' is a helpful reminder to keep me on track with how I plan, design, and implement CPD. Over the years, I have often referred to non-educational books to find better ways of working, and this helps me, as I am sure you have.

Table 4.2 Leading Effective CPD: Applying the Rider and Elephant Analogy to Our Work

The Rider (CPD Leader)	As the rider, we must do the following: • Articulate a well-defined learning pathway for colleagues in our school, avoiding ad hoc and last-minute CPD sessions. • Professional development is for everyone; we can all improve and get better, including all senior leaders! • Plan and implement CPD sessions aligned with reliable evidence. • Emphasise positive aspects and create outstanding learning opportunities. • Demonstrate knowledge of effective CPD, and lead by example, steering clear of educational fads.
The Elephant (Teachers)	As the rider, we must connect with the elephant by doing the following: • Establishing an emotional connection with our colleagues by spelling out the short- and long-term objectives and why this is a key focus for the school. • Offering adequate resources for teachers to be successful and truly enhance their teaching – going beyond the scope of just listening to a series of webinars. • Eliminating judgments and the fear of making mistakes following a CPD activity. • Ensuring our teachers feel a personal investment and empowering them to take ownership of their professional development. • Consistently emphasise the purpose behind our actions. • Conveying the understanding that change is not expected to be instantaneous.

(Continued)

Table 4.2 (Continued)

Shape the Path (Our School/s)	As the rider, we must shape the path by doing the following: • Clearly explaining the expectations of a CPD program/activity, detailing each step and defining everyone's role. • Providing concrete steps, including outlining the specifics of collaboration with colleagues and clearly defining when these collaborative activities will take place. • Allocating time in the school calendar for self-reflection and teaching and learning meet-ups following a CPD activity. • Outlining the methods for assessing and evaluating the work. • Offering coaching and mentoring support. • Ensuring that directed time is used effectively and monitored.

Leading Effective CPD: Applying the Rider and Elephant Analogy to Our Work

Think for a moment about what's happening right now in your school. Are you supporting colleagues in your school to develop their professional practice, or are you actually prohibiting them from doing so (consciously or subconsciously)? As the rider, how are you scanning and searching for the right resources to give your elephant? Precision planning ensures crystal-clear clarity, helping us avoid resistance while finding those ever-so-important bright spots of what's working really well and showcasing how we can just do more of this. There are always so many outstanding best practices right under our noses, so how can we just do more of them so that they are promoted across our school community? These are all important points to consider if we want professional development to be successful and if we want to stick and improve professional practice.

If all of our teachers are well prepared with the right training to develop the habits that we need them to have, a crisis cannot stop our school from improving. However, to achieve this, our colleagues need to feel motivated to continue to practise their habits even when times get tough. So where does human motivation factor into this equation?

Pause for Thought

> How can we use insights from non-educational literature to enrich the planning and delivery of our CPD?

The Power of Motivation to Sustain Good Habits

We all have good and bad days in school. This is normal. But how do you motivate staff day in and day out and keep morale and momentum where it needs to be? This is difficult, especially when we have to deal with challenging parents, a busy term with parent evenings, progress checks and student interventions, and people who are drained and tired. However, this is probably one of the most important areas school leaders need to consider and act on to be successful.

A useful exercise is to refer to Maslow's hierarchy of needs when considering motivation (see Figure 4.2 provided below). This simple theory on human motivation helps me to reflect on what I might be doing to motivate my staff and where we might have fallen behind

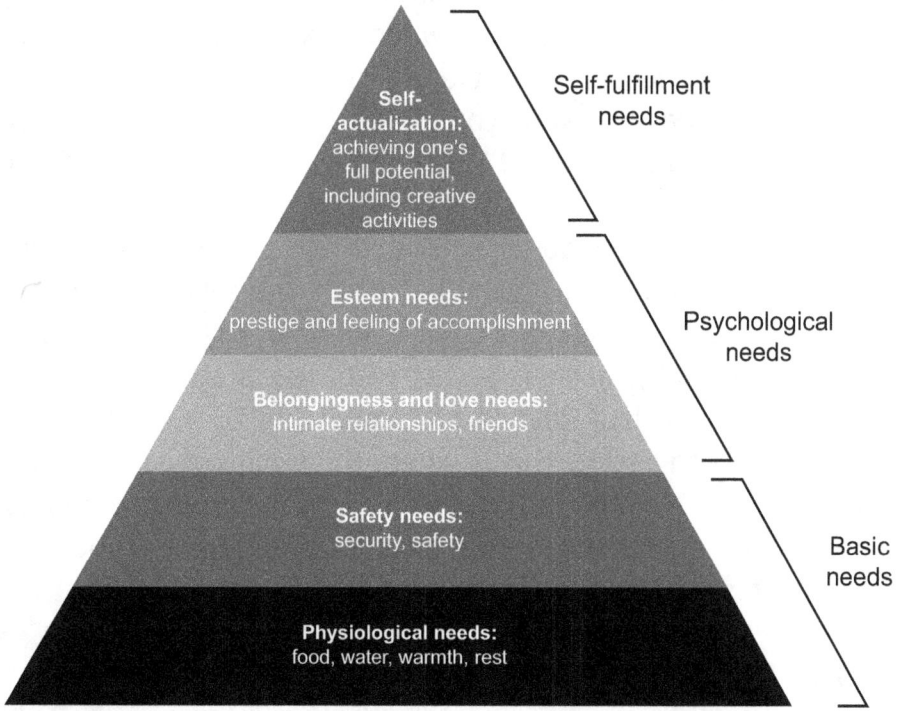

Figure 4.2 Motivating Employees with Maslow's Theory

in some areas. Take a minute now to reflect on this and make notes around the triangle. Perhaps you can also do this with colleagues in your school and compare your answers. This can often be a powerful but effective self-reflection exercise to help us keep on track.

The truth is that employees will only be motivated to continuously work hard if they are happy, feel valued and appreciated, and do not feel judged when they get things wrong or have difficulties. The highest tier in Maslow's (1943) hierarchy is self-actualisation, which is the process of striving to reach one's full potential and achieve self-fulfilment. This entails seeking out personal growth opportunities to become the best version of oneself. Our role as leaders is for staff to reach the self-actualisation stage where they can achieve this. Using the earlier exercise, where are you with this? What are you doing to enable people to realise for themselves their potential and desire to get better and improve?

In schools, for example, where lesson observations are seen as a development exercise, professional development happens with good levels of support where teachers collaborate and staff development reviews are supportive and purposeful. Likewise, we don't motivate people by letting them off the hook when we know they are not following the correct school routines, tolerate rudeness to other colleagues, or are failing in teaching your young people. Not challenging appropriately leads to your best staff becoming demotivated, so having the right balance between support and challenge and choosing what and when you need to challenge appropriately can play a massive role.

Consider for a moment how, if left alone, the following examples can chip away at your school's culture and lead to people becoming demotivated. Initially, of course, our response is that this must be challenged, but the true test of our leadership comes when things become tough and hectic. This is where the reality of our leadership is revealed. How we hold ourselves and others accountable in such situations can significantly impact the culture within our schools and how people respond on the ground.

Scenario 1

A teacher decides to spend departmental time marking a set of tests rather than attend their departmental meeting.

Scenario 2

Teachers are expected to greet students at the door as they enter the classroom, but you notice that a handful of teachers are repeatedly late getting to their lessons and students are left waiting outside.

Scenario 3

As part of directed time, teachers are expected to meet with their coaches and mentors to discuss areas of teaching and learning and pedagogy they are working on improving every five weeks. You've set up the system at the start of term, provided adequate training, and shared the vision. Many staff are on board and doing wonderfully well, and you are seeing improvements in your school. However, a handful of staff are finding opportunities to miss these 60-minute sessions.

Keeping Everyone on Track

Keeping everyone motivated sounds easy in principle. In reality, this can be tough. We all struggle to get this right.

For professional development to be successful, we need to keep staff motivated. Giving the time, space, and support colleagues need to develop professionally is what will make the difference. This is what true investment in people really means and is far more powerful than anything we post on social media, our website, or have laminated in the reception area.

When professional development fails to achieve the desired result, it is often because it has been forced upon staff; they do not see the relevance or the short-term and long-term objectives have not been shared. Therefore, they will not be motivated to either attend, evaluate their own teaching, or adopt more desirable habits.

Neuroscience has captured a lot of attention from educators in recent years, and those who know me well know how much I love learning about the human brain, in particular, undertaking more about cognitive science, learning, and the chemicals the body needs to produce for successful learning to take place.

The Impact of Dopamine on Human Motivation

We know the brain is a complex organ that is responsible for our emotions, behaviours, and motivations. One of the main chemicals associated with motivation is dopamine. When dopamine rises, it increases our motivation and influences our habits or a particular goal we are working towards. It is important for school leaders to understand how this chemical influences teacher motivation so that they are able to effectively support their teachers in their educational journeys and keep them in their 'challenge sweet spots' as is well known by the work of Guy Claxton (2017). If we go too fast or do not provide the right support, then the body will create cortisol which causes anxiety and pushback. I'll explain this in a little more detail.

Dopamine can be released when we are anticipating something pleasurable or when we have achieved a goal. This chemical helps us stay motivated even when times are tough because it rewards us with positive feelings when we reach our goals. It also helps us stick to habits by providing an extra boost of motivation when needed. For example, if you have been studying for an exam, dopamine may be released when you finally finish studying or get a good grade on the test, prompting you to continue studying even though it is difficult at times. Dopamine is also addictive. We want our staff to be addicted to good habits. We need them to feel that their habits are rewarding them regularly.

School leaders need to understand the importance of dopamine effects if they wish to keep their teachers in their 'challenge sweet spots.' A challenge sweet spot (also referred to as the Goldilocks rule) is a place where we work on tasks that are right for us, not too easy not too hard, and where we feel challenged but not overwhelmed. At this level, we are able to grow professionally and develop new skills without feeling overburdened or discouraged. Teachers have access to resources that will help them succeed, such as professional learning opportunities, guidance from more experienced staff members, and guidance materials that can help them stay on track and build good habits. Additionally, school leaders should be aware of how much time teachers are spending on tasks and make sure they aren't feeling overwhelmed or underwhelmed.

But ... Dopamine Isn't the Only Chemical We Need

It is important to remember that dopamine isn't the only chemical we need in order to stay motivated. Other chemicals like serotonin and oxytocin also play an important role in keeping us motivated; for example, serotonin helps regulate our moods, while oxytocin encourages trust and closeness between people. As such, school leaders should strive to create an environment where all these chemicals can be released so that teachers can reach their full potential without feeling overwhelmed or discouraged by the challenges they face. Teaching and learning events, such as 'speed dating,' where teachers come together to talk about pedagogy and what's working or what isn't, staff sharing anonymous problems on a blank canvas in the staffroom, and bite-size professional development events that involve a diverse group of staff members from the school, can foster relationships and provide support.

In the final part of this chapter, I'd like to draw attention to the importance of creating thinking environments and how this can contribute to our professional growth. We know the strong impact teacher collaboration has on developing classroom practice (the same can also be said for developing leadership skills), so giving teachers the space to think is a very powerful component of CPD. It's often not the time someone initially spends in a CPD session but the work that will follow afterwards and the opportunity for self-critique and analysis. By creating thinking environments, we enable our colleagues not only to work together and build positive relationships (most of the time) but also to motivate them to develop successful habits.

Creating 'Thinking' Environments

Jackie Beere (2016), in her book 'Grow – Change Your Mindset, Change Your Life – A Practical Guide To Thinking on Purpose' (which is another one of my must-read recommendations), coins the phrase 'Thinking on Purpose,' which is the idea that we are in control of our thinking by taking a step back and managing our thinking in a rational way. Getting into the habit of doing this will be considering what actions we should or should have taken. This is very similar to the idea of fast and slow thinking by Daniel Kahneman in 'Thinking, Fast and Slow' (2013), where Kahneman explains that fast thinking is often intuitive, automatic, and spontaneous. This is often a result of the type of action we see when teachers take in the classroom when dealing with student behaviour or an incident that requires you to act quickly. This is not a bad thing, but the opposite of this is slow thinking. Slow thinking requires deep concentration and thought and is an opportunity for us to stand back and manage our thinking. When it comes to giving teachers time, professional development activities should include slow thinking in part of the design stages of any programme. Opportunities to think critically and be challenged are important components of professional growth. Allowing time for practitioners to reframe their thinking and providing a clear opportunity to unpick stuff on a deeper level is a step in the right direction for supporting better classroom practice. Again, by failing to do this, we are limiting the chances for professional learning to be successful, and therefore, our time, efforts, and the money we spend will be wasted.

Nancy Kline (1999) has famously coined the phrase 'thinking environments' from her book 'Time to Think' (if you are interested more about Nancy's work, take some time a look at the Time to Think website: https://www.timetothink.com/). I'll be coming back a bit more on this in Chapter 7 when we'll be discussing coaching and the impact this has on CPD. However, I wanted to mention this here, as creating thinking environments is a very powerful tool for enabling colleagues to come together to talk, question, and realise their potential. This can be achieved in our schools through coaching, the development of teaching and learning communities, and regular time-to-think meetings that are part of any CPD programme. Creating a thinking environment shows you value your staff's expertise by giving them this space to think about their professional practice. It could be argued that there is nothing more important than this. If you don't provide opportunities for teachers to come together and think about pedagogy outside of the classroom, then this is something that needs to be looked at. And FAST!

Tweaking the School Environment to Support Professional Learning

As you've probably gathered, I'm a lover of small steps, and the evidence in this thinking supports my approach. Small actions can have a massive impact, sometimes on a subconscious level. That's why I believe tweaking our school environment and making things really visible can really help us reinforce key concepts and ideas that we want everyone to try out.

- **Staffroom CPD goodies**
  Bring your staffrooms to life by providing bite-size, up-to-date professional development resources that can be easily accessed and read by all staff. Include subject-specific resources and invite staff during school INSETs, twilights, and whole-school meetings to talk about their key learning points inviting questions from colleagues. Try not to make this taxing of people's time. Teachers are busy, and we shouldn't be adding to their workloads, so we need to do this in a way that teachers have access to high-quality resources and at the same time are able to apply this in the best way possible. CPD postcards, a couple of reflection questions, a blog recommendation, or a podcast are perfectly sufficient in my opinion.
- **Promoting pedagogical discussions in meetings**
  Pedagogical topics should be a standard item on every departmental meeting agenda. While it may be challenging to do so consistently, discussing teaching and learning is essential. I recommend incorporating this into the agenda at least every four weeks to encourage sharing and conversation about pedagogy and best practices. Furthermore, it's highly valuable to make it a requirement for any department or whole-school meeting following a school INSET or twilight session where everyone has gathered. This not only reinforces what's been covered but also allows staff to engage and discuss their experiences. You can get creative by showcasing video snapshots of teachers in action (with their approval and if they're willing). Embedding this as a standard protocol after any whole-staff training has proven to work effectively.

- **Lesson observations**
  I could write a lot about this, but for the purpose of how we make this work for successful CPD that supports teachers' development, I think it's fairly obvious. They need to be low stakes, where teachers feel invited to really dig deep and pull parts of the teaching to bits. This is where a more highly experienced teacher comes in and has such a powerful role to play. Capturing this on video, in my opinion, is fab CPD, as it facilitates successful conversations. However, this should only ever be used for the purpose of a teacher reflecting on their teaching and not to judge the quality of teaching. If you have this mindset, bin it!

- **Good communication is seen, not just heard**
  Think about how you communicate the message of CPD across your schools. Do the actions of everyone in the school support your culture on staff development? Think about the non-verbal communication you use towards CPD and the message you portray. Our aim should be to build a culture where everyone in our school can get better and improve, and people see this. This comes from the top, so ensuring that everyone can see this is so important both in our written and in non-written communication with staff. People often gravitate to the law of the least effort, so we want to ensure we prohibit this as much as possible. If staff know that this is just another training session and there is no further follow-up, then this will just occur time and time again. To avoid this, we must make sure we communicate the expectations we have of staff when it comes to professional learning, what's involved, and what they'll be doing (with their input driving this change).

- **The dreaded performance management**
  Let's be honest. Depending on what school you work in, the experience of this can be so different, which really shouldn't be the case. Have we overcomplicated this that, in reality, we hinder its effectiveness? If we are going to make CPD a success, then I firmly believe we need to really look at whether performance management is working for our staff or actually against them. I would encourage you to really look at your performance development

review cycle to make sure that they sit side by side with what the CPD individuals need to engage with. Support should be clear and evidenced. CPD should support staff performance development or professional growth plans (as some schools now refer to), and this should include purposeful reflection at different points of the year.

- **Shouting it from the rooftops!**
Every corner of your school should promote the expertise of your staff and celebrate what you've achieved and how far you've come. Make this visible across the school with clear reminders of what this looks like so that everyone can see it. This might be captured on video and showcased around the school or simply a visual reminder near a teacher's desk on the area teaching they are working on. Often known as the nudge effect, we want to point people in the right direction to ensure that there are helpful reminders around the school of what we are working towards.

The Four Stages of Competence by Noel Burch

For those of you familiar with the competence model, I find it a valuable psychological framework that explains how we become both competent and confident in successfully using new skills (a visual illustration of the model is provided later, Figure 4.3). For example, at the beginning of a professional development programme, we often find ourselves at the 'unconscious incompetent' stage. At this stage, people are not aware of what they don't know, and quite often, this is a very comfortable place to be. We then move on to the conscious incompetence stage. At this stage, we have the knowledge, and learning begins, but we have not mastered it. At this stage, things can go two ways. You can be encouraged to move forward to the next stage, 'unconscious competence,' which requires hard work, conscious thought, and practice to move onto stage 4, 'conscious competence.' On the contrary, when we fail to have the right resources or support, we'll often do nothing with this new learning and revert to stage 1, the unconscious incompetent stage. This is so important to bear in mind, as it is psychological models like this that will help us fine-tune our CPD programmes.

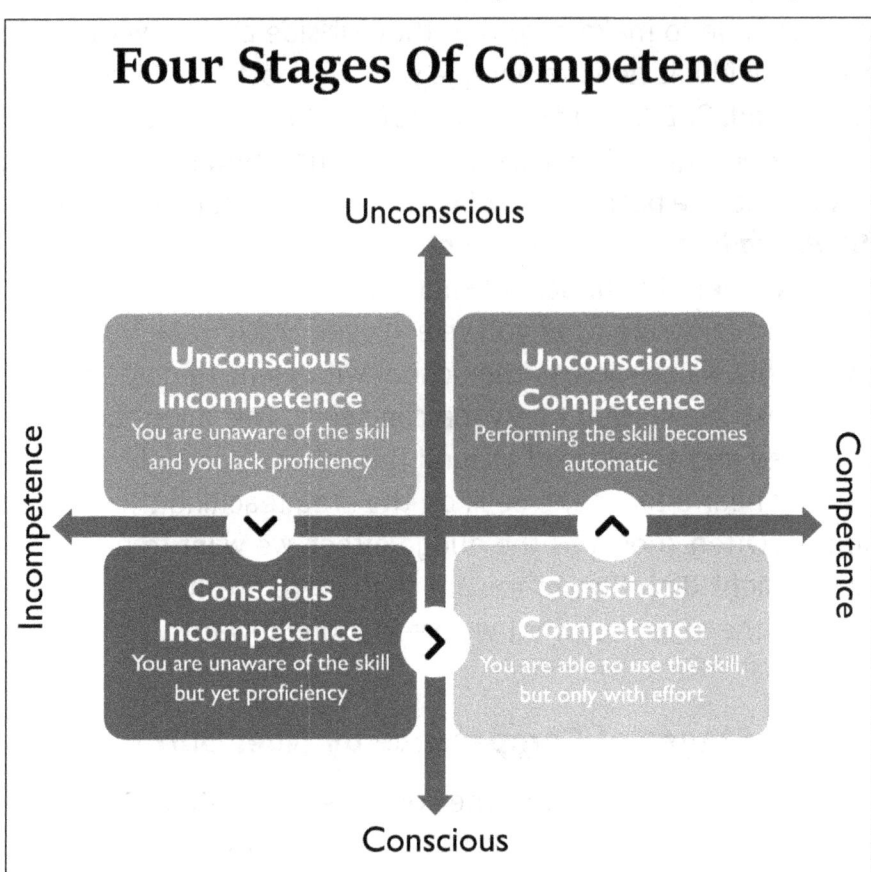

Figure 4.3 The Four Stages of Competence

How we encourage people to move from conscious incompetence to conscious competence is where the challenge lies for us CPD leaders, and it's where the hard work begins. The ideas covered in the next chapter and those mentioned earlier and in Table 4.1 should help and get you thinking.

The learning environment we create towards CPD can really make a difference. It does in the schools that I work with, and it is often the little quick things we do that can shift mindsets and give people the tools they need to be successful. For professional development activities to stick, perhaps it's wise we carry out a

CPD health audit on our schools to see whether we are in the right place. Sounds easy, but in reality, this is where we go wrong. Making simple but effective changes to your environment can dramatically change the success of a professional development programme, INSET, or seminar.

Conclusion

This chapter has explored how important it is for teachers to have the right habits in place. As a leader, it is our job to create the conditions for those habits to form and how we improve teaching through purposeful practice and effective feedback.

Understanding the psychology behind building effective habits is of equal importance. We must keep teachers excited and motivated to work hard towards improving their classroom teaching, not because we are not good but because we can be even better (Dylan William). Teachers also need the time to reflect, refine, and evaluate their teaching as part of any professional development activity they engage with. If we are going to expect the best from our teachers, as we do for our students, then we need to create the suitable environments and conditions for them to improve. CPD, often judged as poor and unsatisfactory, comes down to a lack of careful planning with no time opportunity for staff to experiment and the time given to trial new ideas. This is a detriment to any professional development we offer practitioners, so we need to really think about this as we design CPD that has an impact and supports teachers in developing their craft and building effective habits. Taking into account lessons from leadership outside of education, neuroscience, and the science of building habits that stick (and breaking the bad ones) can really help us when we are thinking about how to improve the quality of CPD in our schools. In the next chapter, we will look at the different types of CPD activities we have in schools and provide some ideas about how we can get the best out of them, marrying all the concepts we have discussed so far in the book.

Reflective Questions

1. Are you a school that focuses more on goals rather than systems to improve individual performance?
2. How can the time we have available for CPD work in our favour and against us?
3. How do you give staff in your school the time to practice new knowledge and skills they've acquired from a professional development programme?
4. What inhibits someone from developing professionally in your school? What are you doing about this?
5. How do you use deliberate practice to develop teachers' knowledge and skills within the classroom?
6. How do you keep your staff motivated and in their Goldilocks zone?
7. What do high support and high challenge look like in your school?
8. How would you build into your professional development the concept of atomic habits?
9. Do we really not have the time in schools to offer this level of support to teachers? Should we sack our bad teachers and replace them with better ones?
10. Reflection and review enable you to remain conscious of your performance. How do you create thinking environments where everyone recognises the value of their own thinking?

Chapter Snapshots

- CPD initiatives can often fail in schools due to insufficient time for delivery and evaluation. Quick fixes and tick-box CPD rarely yield overnight miracles.
- The pandemic has shown us the agility we can achieve and how to leverage this advantage when considering school improvement and change.
- Embedding the principles of building effective habits can have a dual positive impact: enhancing the quality of a CPD programme and increasing its chances of success.

- Knowing how to implement deliberate practice is a powerful vehicle to develop teachers' skills and expertise, guided by a set of principles. The concept of deliberate practice was given to us by Anders Ericsson in his book 'Peak - Secrets from the New Science of Expertise.'
- Achieving mastery in skills and expertise involves three key elements: establishing effective systems in schools to cultivate teaching habits, inspiring and enabling staff to reach their full potential for growth and excellence, and implementing manageable changes that ensure success.
- The concept of marginal gains is crucial. Tiny daily improvements can significantly enhance performance over time. Our CPD model should incorporate this mindset, along with essential steps and resources for teachers to succeed in any CPD activity.
- Make the new habit attractive enough for teachers to willingly adopt it. A supportive, non-judgmental culture with ample praise for those striving to improve is essential. CPD should offer opportunities for learning in this manner.
- Ensure that your teachers, like students, receive the right dopamine 'fixes' they need to be successful learners.
- Employees will remain motivated if they are happy, feel valued, and don't fear judgment when facing challenges or making mistakes. Using Maslow's hierarchy of needs as a tool for keeping staff motivated provides valuable insights to us CPD leaders responsible for shaping how CPD is implemented in our schools.
- How do you use non-educational literature to design, plan, and implement CPD? Chip Heath and Dan Heath (2011) emphasises the emotional connection between the rational part of our brain (the rider) and the emotional side (the elephant) for successful change.
- Tweaking our school environment can be highly beneficial for teacher learning. Creating an environment that brings staffrooms to life and effectively utilising teacher collaboration, lesson observations, and meetings can have a very positive impact on building effective habits with lasting change.

References

Beere, J. (2016) *Grow: Change your mindset, change your life*. Williston, VT: Crown House Publishing.

Claxton, G. (2017) *The learning power approach: Teaching learners to teach themselves*. Thousand Oaks, CA: Corwin.

Clear, J. (2018) *Atomic habits: Tiny changes, remarkable results: An easy & proven way to build good habits & break bad ones*. London: Random House Business Books.

Coe, R. (2020) 'The case for subject-specific CPD', in *Institute of physics CPD summit*. London: Institute of Physics. Available at: https://www.iop.org/sites/default/files/2022-05/the-case-for-subject-specific-cpd-robert-coe.pdf.

Deans for Impact (2016) 'Practice with purpose: The emerging science of teaching expertise', *Deans for Impact*. Available at: https://www.deansforimpact.org/files/assets/practice-with-purpose.pdf.

Heath, C. and Heath, D. (2011) *Switch: How to change things when change is hard*. London: Random House Business.

Kahneman, D. (2013) *Thinking, fast and slow*. First paperback edition. New York: Farrar, Straus and Giroux.

Kline, N. (1999) *Time to think: Listening to ignite the human mind*. London: Ward Lock.

Kraft, M. and Papay, J. (2017) 'Developing workplaces where teachers stay, improve, and succeed', in E. Quintero (ed) *Teaching in context: The social side of education reform* (pp. 15-35). Cambridge, MA: Harvard Education Press.

Leading schools through the COVID-19 pandemic – Insights from school leaders around the world (2021). Available at: https://www.youtube.com/watch?v=JGP2BOAFb6Q.

Maslow, A.H. (1943) 'A theory of human motivation', *Psychological Review*, 50, pp.370-396.

5 How to Plan and Deliver Effective Teacher CPD

Research indicates that teachers tend to require tangible proof of the effectiveness of a new teaching method or innovation before they are willing to fully commit to it long-term (Guskey, 2002). If we cannot see it effectively benefiting our students, we simply won't adopt it. This visible proof, particularly regarding its impact on students' achievements, is the crucial catalyst for change. Once this validation has been established, the new approach can be integrated into your teaching practice and continue to yield benefits in terms of student performance.

Collaborating with fellow educators who are also implementing these strategies is particularly beneficial in scenarios involving the entire school, when multiple teachers have participated in the same professional development, or when a staff member has returned and shared their experiences.

This chapter will help you to explore the following areas:

- The framework I follow when planning and delivering effective CPD.
- Different types of CPD activities and what we might consider as well as what to avoid when planning school INSET days, twilight sessions, workshops, Teachmeets, online CPD, and educational conferences.
- How to deal with disengaged or challenging people who might not see the point of being there!
- Maximise your potential with the 'C' for continuing professional development.

Crafting top-notch continuous professional development (CPD) ensures that teachers thrive in the process and remain motivated and engaged due to its relevance. To craft excellent CPD requires a blend of key ingredients:

- Directly relevant to the school's needs
- Tailored to meet the needs of an individual and their desired areas of improvement
- Modern educational content
- Seamless delivery methods
- Effective assessment activities
- Meaningful reflection opportunities
- Follow-up and next steps

As a leader of learning in a busy educational establishment, you can be so squeezed for time that CPD doesn't always get the attention it deserves. It can be very difficult, even more so if you are in a small school with limited resources and funds. We know that CPD is the most powerful tool for improving staff morale and retention, so we must plan to avoid putting the creation of the best possible CPD last on our lists.

Five Vital Musts

When planning any type of teacher CPD, there are five vital components that we must consider and applies to all:

1. Ensure you know your audience very well and involve them in the planning stage. You can ask them to complete a short questionnaire to gauge their thoughts and complete a very short pretraining activity to observe their understanding of key ideas and what they are hoping to get out of the PD. You can also gain knowledge about what they do not want. There is nothing worse than presenting material that is not relevant to your audience or presenting content that does not stretch and challenge.
2. Learning outcomes need to be clear for each part of the CPD activity. Where necessary, connect the learning outcomes of the

training to the overall learning aims and objectives of longer programme, and be clear about what will be achieved at each stage. It is important to refer to this particularly at the beginning of the training session and at the end.

3. A CPD activity should be planned with a follow-up in mind. No one should leave the room without knowing what to do next. This is one of my mantras. There is no use in completing a reflection activity if nothing happens afterwards. Follow-ups should be clear, actionable, and presented as a whole-school approach. I have found Kolb's (2015) experiential learning theory to be a vital element of any CPD plan. We should use this when considering how we, as practitioners, engage in purposeful reflection. I've provided a brief overview of Kolb's theory later in Figure 5.1.

4. Research-based approach: I've incorporated a significant amount of educational research throughout each chapter because referencing research evidence is crucial. It's essential to draw on research while also striking a balance with our daily practices to ensure effective time and workload management. It's important to bear in mind that many academics may not have practical experience in a classroom setting. Professional development should not be undertaken without a solid theoretical foundation. It is crucial to support professional development with evidence-based approaches. However, simply presenting teachers with new research findings is not enough, and it is not enough just to give them a list of practical strategies to try out without the evidence given as to why this works within the classroom.

Additionally, I have already provided a case of the positive impact that arises when teachers are given ample opportunities for engaging in dialogue, problem-solving, and questioning to understand how these approaches fit into their school context. As the people working in our schools daily, I would like to believe that we possess valuable insights and an understanding of what is needed, which is why it is important to invest time in aligning their ideas with the strongest research available.

80 A School Leader's Guide to Leading Professional Development

5. Participants mustn't be merely passive listeners. The activities you plan should make participants think hard. It is vital to foster active participant engagement and involvement, encouraging them to actively contribute and participate in the learning process. Excessive text on a slide is not helpful, and reading directly from the slide should be avoided. Instead, focus on facilitating meaningful discussions and identifying any gaps in learning or understanding. Participants should have a clear understanding of the purpose behind your delivery of the sessions, as well as your area of expertise. How you present your material is essential; your tone of voice, confidence, and communication with the audience can make or break your session. However, WHAT participants are doing is even more important than that.

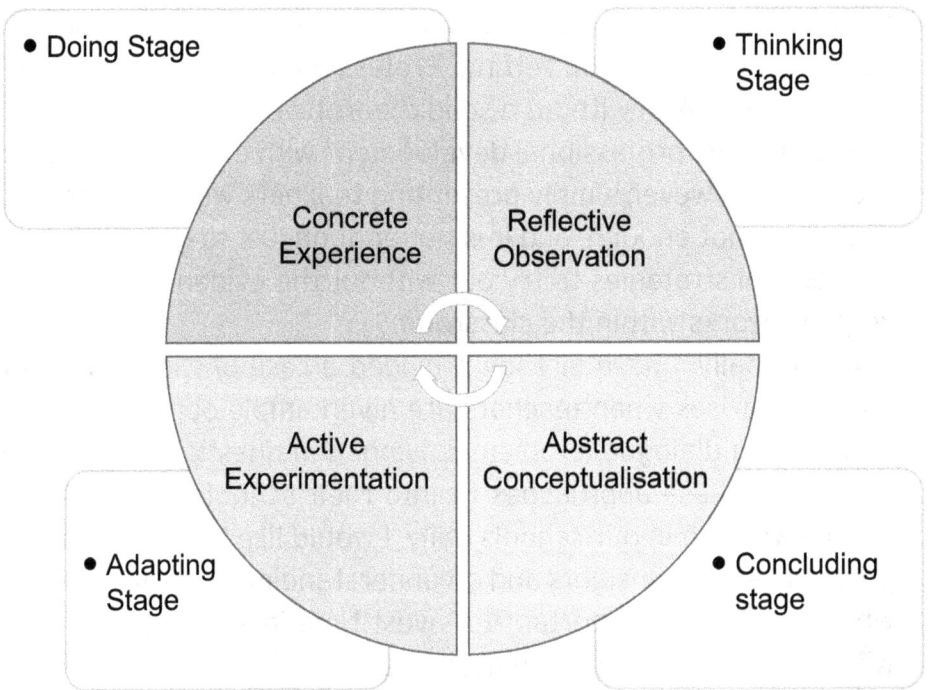

Figure 5.1 Kolb's Reflective Cycle

Before we explore the various types of CPD training conducted in our schools, let's establish some common threads that should be woven into all forms of professional development.

Clear Learning Objectives and Outcomes

Ensure that the training has well-defined learning objectives and clearly stated outcomes. This provides a clear direction for participants and allows them to gauge their progress throughout the session. Think: What are they learning? Why are they learning that?

Rigorous Challenge Appropriate to the Audience

Tailor the level of challenge in the training to suit the audience. As the expert, you are there with the knowledge they need. As educated professionals, they have knowledge too. Don't ignore this. Know your audience and adapt the content and delivery to ensure it is appropriately challenging for participants.

Bite-Size Information and Connection to Previous Learning

Present information in bite-size portions, making connections to participants' prior knowledge and previous learning experiences. This helps learners build upon what they already know and facilitates better retention and understanding.

Purposeful Activities With a Focus on Learning

Design activities that serve a clear purpose beyond mere entertainment. Instead of focusing solely on fun, ensure that the activities are purposeful and directly contribute to the learning goals of the session. I don't mean to sound like a buzzkill, but meaningful engagement is key!

Marrying Up-Research With Real-Life Practical Classroom Strategies

Integrate the latest educational research findings and use practical examples from real-life school settings. Provide participants with a toolbox of ideas that are not only backed by research evidence but also demonstrate how they can be applied effectively and why they work.

Reflection Points and Sharing Best Practices

Include designated reflection points throughout the training, allowing participants to reflect on their own practices and share best practices with one another. This fosters a collaborative learning environment and encourages the exchange of valuable insights and experiences from both classrooms and schools.

Establishing Key Commitments and Next Steps

Wrap up the training by identifying key commitments and outlining what actions will be taken next. Paint a vivid picture of how participants can apply their newly acquired knowledge and skills in their own contexts, ensuring that they leave with a clear plan of action and an understanding of how this will be followed up.

Take a minute or two to reflect upon your own thinking about professional development. Reflect on the following questions:

Pause for Thought
1. When attending a CPD session/s, what do you appreciate taking part in?
2. When designing CPD, what activities do you incorporate that work well?
3. What have you tried in the past that did not work?

Answering these questions ourselves allows us to look first from the participant's point of view and critically examine the factors that we already know contribute to successful professional development. It also provides an opportunity to identify potential pitfalls and unproductive practices that we should be mindful of.

Teacher Appreciation of Your Session

First and foremost, it is essential to recognise that professional development should extend beyond creating a feel-good or inspirational atmosphere. While it is undoubtedly beneficial to inspire participants (and put a smile on their faces), the aim of CPD should be to foster growth and progress in our thinking and practice. Rather than focusing solely on eliciting positive emotions, it is more valuable to encourage open and honest dialogue, enabling participants to share their thoughts, concerns, and ideas freely. This requires you to be prepared! Know your content, and be ready for difficult questions that may arise.

Engaging in a thoughtful exchange of ideas allows us to understand how the content being presented aligns with the participant's current thinking and practice. By actively discussing and exploring the relevance of new concepts, we can address the challenges that educators face in implementing change and seek strategies to overcome them. It is crucial to create an environment where participants feel comfortable expressing their opinions and grappling with the complexities of their professional roles.

Ultimately, the success of professional development lies in providing teachers with new skills, knowledge, and behaviours for meaningful growth opportunities, challenging established practices, and empowering teachers to embrace change. By doing this, we can ensure that CPD serves as a catalyst for continuous improvement in teaching and learning and that ongoing engagement is maintained.

Delivery Methods

While we certainly want our audience to have an enjoyable experience, it is important to remember that the substance of the CPD content and the delivery methods employed hold paramount significance. The content should be carefully curated to address the specific needs and interests of the participants, grounded in current research and experiential-based practices. It should go beyond surface-level engagement and provide opportunities for deep reflection and skill development.

Delivery methods do not simply need to be your direct input. They can be diverse and interactive, incorporating a range of instructional strategies such as the following:

- Collaborative group work
- Case studies/scenarios

- Hands-on activities
- Role-play modelling exercises

These methods can be used to encourage active participation and critical thinking, enabling educators to apply the new knowledge and skills to their own contexts. Consider what you want participants to learn and decide the best way to engage with that knowledge.

Simplified CPD: Frameworks for Effortless Planning and Deliver

Before planning professional development sessions, I always make sure that I have referred to useful frameworks such as the model of great teaching by evidence-based education, 'Teach Like a Champion' by Doug Lemov (2021), and Rosenshine's 'Principles of Instruction' (2012). Such publications are helpful in delivering new content to students, and how we teach students is closely aligned with how adults learn. Therefore, I adopt a similar approach when planning CPD training, basing my thinking, ideas, and approach on how I would plan a lesson or a series of lessons. I particularly love the Great Teaching Toolkit by Evidence-Based Education, the Education Endowment Foundation (Coe et al., 2020) for reliable, up-to-date, research-based teaching pedagogies, and the work of Dylan William in this area, as they provide clear structural guidance to deliver content in a way that will help our audience to learn. Let's look more closely at one example to see how this works in reality.

A Model of Great Teaching by Evidence-Based Education

We will examine how we can adapt and use this model provided by Evidence-Based Education when planning professional development sessions, but it is important to note, as Dylan William has well documented, that many strategies can be effective in education. The key is to discover what works most effectively for your students and to implement more of those methods. I don't believe there is a one-size-fits-all approach, so let's keep this in mind when structuring and planning professional development for our colleagues. We should focus on planning CPD that meets our staff's specific wants and needs, rather than simply following trends or what other schools might be doing.

The model for great teaching examines evidence-based teaching practices that impact student performance. It consists of 17 elements organised into four dimensions. If you are not familiar with this, then take a look at Figure 5.2 for a brief explanation of each element:

1. Understanding Content

This emphasises the importance of teachers having excellent subject knowledge, identifying the common misconceptions and difficulties students may face while teaching, understanding how the curriculum is sequenced, drawing on connections, and using the right assessments and activities to assess learning.

2. Creating a Supportive Environment

This includes developing and promoting good relationships based on respect and understanding and setting high expectations for learning, where learners feel they can learn from their mistakes.

3. Maximising the Opportunity to Learn

This includes promoting and using good learning routines so that time is not wasted. Behavioural consequences are clear and explicit, with responses being preventive and reactive when necessary, along with clear instructions.

4. Activating Hard Thinking

Evidence-based strategies, such as explicit teaching, questioning techniques, and feedback, help challenge thinkers and expand and help students become independent thinkers and experts.

As a CPD leader, I use the Great Teaching Toolkit when planning a CPD session because it provides a checklist that I know supports teacher development. For example, I always make sure of the following:

- Participants always understand how the subject matter relates to their own subject area. CPD time is given to develop subject knowledge and subject-specific pedagogies.
- Participants develop a deep understanding of why the strategies presented in a CPD session are effective and how they help students achieve.
- Activities are appropriate, and time is well-spent, covering material that they already know.
- There is modelling and scaffolding of new ideas to support teachers in implementing these concepts in the classroom.
- Activities that support positive learning environments that bring teachers together, initiating productive discussions.
- Appropriate feedback that helps teachers embed new skills, with an emphasis on open-ended questions.

Further CPD tools to help teachers enhance their practice are available to view at https://evidencebased.education/a-model-for-great-teaching/.

Considering these ideas and referring to the earlier as a checklist, let's explore the various types of professional development activities we engage with as teachers, identifying the key components essential for success and what can be avoided.

CPD Programmes

I'm starting with CPD programmes because this is the best form of professional development. By designing a good CPD programme, you can really begin to work with a school or practitioner to develop their practice.

What Makes a Great CPD Programme?

- Any long-term objectives are shared at the start of the programme.
- The short-term objectives are shared every step of the way and linked to the longer-term objectives.
- Content is bespoke and fully personalised.
- The delivery methods take a variety of approaches: in-person, online, in-class support, observations. Be creative here, as there is

How to Plan and Deliver Effective Teacher CPD 87

A Model for **Great Teaching**

1. Understanding the content

1 Having deep and fluent knowledge and flexible understanding of the content you are teaching

2 Knowledge of the requirements of curriculum sequencing and dependencies in relation to the content and ideas you are teaching

3 Knowledge of relevant curriculum tasks, assessments and activities, their diagnostic and didactic potential; being able to generate varied explanations and multiple representations/analogies/examples for the ideas you are teaching

4 Knowledge of common student strategies, misconceptions and sticking points in relation to the content you are teaching

2. Creating a supportive environment

1 Promoting interactions and relationships with all students that are based on mutual respect, care, empathy and warmth; avoiding negative emotions in interactions with students; being sensitive to the individual needs, emotions, culture and beliefs of students

2 Promoting a positive climate of student-student relationships, characterised by respect, trust, cooperation and care

3 Promoting learner motivation through feelings of competence, autonomy and relatedness

4 Creating a climate of high expectations, with high challenge and high trust, so learners feel it is okay to have a go; encouraging learners to attribute their success or failure to things they can change

3. Maximising opportunity to learn

1 Managing time and resources efficiently in the classroom to maximise productivity and minimise wasted time (e.g., starts, transitions); giving clear instructions so students understand what they should be doing; using (and explicitly teaching) routines to make transitions smooth

2 Ensuring that rules, expectations and consequences for behaviour are explicit, clear and consistently applied

3 Preventing, anticipating & responding to potentially disruptive incidents; reinforcing positive student behaviours; signalling awareness of what is happening in the classroom and responding appropriately

4. Activating hard thinking

1 Structuring: giving students an appropriate sequence of learning tasks; signalling learning objectives, rationale, overview, key ideas and stages of progress; matching tasks to learners' needs and readiness; scaffolding and supporting to make tasks accessible to all, but gradually removed so that all students succeed at the required level

2 Explaining: presenting and communicating new ideas clearly, with concise, appropriate, engaging explanations; connecting new ideas to what has previously been learnt (and re-activating/checking that prior knowledge); using examples (and non-examples) appropriately to help learners understand and build connections; modelling/demonstrating new skills or procedures with appropriate scaffolding and challenge; using worked/part-worked examples

3 Questioning: using questions and dialogue to promote elaboration and connected, flexible thinking among learners (e.g., 'Why?', 'Compare', etc.); using questions to elicit student thinking; getting responses from all students; using high-quality assessment to evidence learning; interpreting, communicating and responding to assessment evidence appropriately

4 Interacting: responding appropriately to feedback from students about their thinking/knowledge/understanding; giving students actionable feedback to guide their learning

5 Embedding: giving students tasks that embed and reinforce learning; requiring them to practise until learning is fluent and secure; ensuring that once-learnt material is reviewed/revisited to prevent forgetting

6 Activating: helping students to plan, regulate and monitor their own learning; progressing appropriately from structured to more independent learning as students develop knowledge and expertise

Evidence Based Education   **Great Teaching** Toolkit   greatteaching.com

Figure 5.2 Summary Poster 'A Model for Great Teaching' by Evidence-Based Education

so much we can do. A combination of all these things, throughout, can be really powerful in a person's learning journey and can really impact whether the objectives we've set will be met or need to be adapted further.

- It is spread over a period of time to enable ongoing support, whether this includes coaching, mentoring, or the collaboration of staff. Remember that more effective professional development lasts between two to three terms.
- Go back on material often. Don't assume that just because something has been covered once it has been mastered. Think about how what we know leads to mastery learning for our students. Our role when designing CPD programmes is not just about giving knowledge to the focus on enhancing practice.
- CPD programmes should include collaboration and be agreed upon at each stage. Those leading the CPD should ensure this is happening and assess learning along the way.
- Be open to change and for new things to flow organically. We might agree on a particular programme, but along the way, this is likely to change as new things come up. Although we will be guided by the programme schedule, we won't let this be too prescriptive for us.
- Explain what each next step will be followed, for example, a smaller PD activity, what should be followed, and when. I think it is very important to set key dates and commitments at each stage of the CPD programme and hold people to account.
- Evaluation plays a pivotal role in the success of the CPD programme. Work out at each key milestone how things are going (don't leave this for just the end, as it cannot often be too late to know what is working and what needs changing). Ask for feedback on whether this is a short questionnaire or survey and not just from the participants involved but also their line managers or coaches if applicable. Avoid this being just from one person. When you get to Chapter 7, the evaluation of CPD, using the example questionnaires I have provided, will help you.
- Celebrate successes and showcase this across the school. We can do this throughout a CPD programme. Not only can we share best practices but we can also really document a person's development,

and how we do this should be documented during the planning process of the CPD programme. For example, you could also ask the person to put together a short video or what they've achieved so far and what they are working on. This can then be shared with other colleagues in the school. Or if you do not want this to be too taxing, they could simply share their learning path during a staff briefing or whole-school meeting.

What You Should Avoid

- **One-size-fits-all approach:** Avoid adopting a generic approach that fails to address individual teachers' specific needs and contexts. Tailoring the programme to the unique requirements of participants increases engagement and relevance.
- **Lack of clarity and objectives:** Ensure that the programme's goals, objectives, and expected outcomes are clearly communicated to participants. Vague or ambiguous objectives can lead to confusion and hinder the overall effectiveness of the CPD programme.
- **Overloading the schedule:** Be mindful of overwhelming participants with a jam-packed programme. We know the impact of cognitive overload, so really think about what you are asking your audience to do. Focus on providing essential and practical knowledge, allowing teachers to absorb and apply what they have learned effectively. Ensure the school has all the relevant resources in place that will ensure the professional development programme is a success. It is not just about the person's commitment. If the system is not set up to support the person to achieve, then the CPD programme won't work.
- **Insufficient Support:** A successful CPD programme includes ongoing support and 'pause-for-thought' moments. Avoid neglecting intersession activities, coaching, or mentoring, as these elements are vital for translating CPD into sustained improvements in teaching practice. Set specific dates from the start so that participants know what to expect even if things change. They set a precedent.
- **Lack of participant engagement:** Actively involve participants throughout the CPD programme to enhance their engagement. Incorporate interactive activities, foster group discussions, and

include practical exercises to encourage active participation with both the facilitator and their peers.
- **Ignoring feedback and evaluation:** Neglecting feedback and evaluation mechanisms can hinder the programme's ability to adapt and improve. Regularly gather feedback from participants and other stakeholders to identify areas of strength and areas that require modification.
- **Professional feedback** must be about improving the individuals' performance and not about providing their capabilities – feedback that is fully individualised and personal to their needs and sets a clear road map for success.

Pause for Thought
- Which of my best practices do you currently implement?
- Which ones would you like to embrace further, and what strategies could you employ to achieve this?
- Are there any of these practices that would not work or be suitable for your specific school context when designing and planning a CPD programme? If so, what are the reasons behind their infeasibility or lack of suitability?

INSET Days: Making Every Moment Count!

When it comes to INSET (In-Service Education and Training) days, they should only be undertaken if there is a clear vision of the training's purpose and the desired outcomes for the school. Our investment of time and resources demands that INSET days are meticulously planned, meaningful, and directly relevant. INSET days have the potential to be better planned and delivered. After all, time is a precious commodity, and we must make the most of every minute. This has become another mantra!

Essentials for INSET Days!

- Ensure effective planning for all your INSET days throughout the academic year, like planning a CPD programme, aligning the focus of these days with school improvement goals, and providing opportunities for all stakeholders to contribute and participate. Early on, CPD leaders should communicate the intended focus of INSET days, allowing staff to share their opinions and insights. This presents a valuable opportunity to identify any overlooked aspects. Similarly, your school CPD calendar with all your CPD listings and provisions should be tied into your INSET days and made public to everyone at least a term ahead if not for the entire school year. Many schools now create a CPD menu or catalogue for staff to choose what professional development they will engage in. This is fab but must be created with teacher input and from senior leaders. These ensure PD sessions are in line with any whole-staff INSET training and key priorities set on the school improvement plans.

- **Encourage staff to contribute** to the planning of INSETs. Foster a collaborative environment where those in leadership positions do not solely dictate best practices. This approach cultivates the desired professional learning culture, as colleagues of all levels and experiences can share valuable knowledge. In the schools I work with, when this is done very well, it really boosts staff morale.
- **Practical tips** are only helpful if we know why they work so well. For example, teachers should be encouraged to critique any classroom strategy and make it their own to suit their learner's needs. This should be encouraged during an INSET training event, and practitioners must understand why something works so well with the evidence behind it.
- While outside subject specialists can be beneficial, relying solely on them is insufficient. Outside trainers can bring fresh perspectives and prevent narrow-mindedness. In my early days of delivering training, I often conducted stand-alone INSET days, as I learnt that schools are likely to invest in ongoing CPD programmes with familiarity with the trainer and their values. Any external INSET training should complement and advance the existing practices within the school. I recall an INSET day when Dylan William delivered training years ago, which was valuable, but we did not maximise its potential due to insufficient consideration of our school's context and plans for utilising the training. Therefore, it falls upon school leaders to establish clarity on how the INSET day will sup-

port staff improvement, set expectations for everyone, and ensure alignment with previous training. By doing this, our staff will recognise the purpose and value of these events, rather than perceive them as just another routine INSET day or expressing reservations like 'It was good, BUT.'

- Ensure active participation from all attendees during INSET days. Everyone must leave the day knowing how to implement new ideas and apply their learning in practical ways. Remember, the purpose of professional learning is not just to enhance our knowledge but also to make a tangible impact on our daily practices. Encourage feedback, whether it is gathered during the day or a few days afterwards, and ensure that everyone understands what steps they need to take next. If something didn't go as planned during an INSET day, take the time to identify the issue, and take appropriate action to address it.
- Consider the next steps in the context of strategic planning and involve all senior leaders. Planning outstanding INSET days should not be the sole responsibility of CPD leaders; the entire school community should be involved. This collaborative approach provides a valuable opportunity for learning and accountability.

What You Should Avoid

Stand-alone INSETs: Avoid conducting INSET training without aligning the learning outcomes with the school's working practices and culture. It is so important to establish a common thread throughout the INSET days, even if adjustments are made along the way. This ensures that staff, either individually or as departments, take ownership of their goals for the INSET day. Failing to do so questions the professional learning culture we have in our schools and limits staff engagement. I've been invited to schools where I've been introduced to staff and had a lack of engagement from senior leaders. If this happens, think about what this is saying to your staff. Great school leaders (of whom I am lucky to work with so many) model how we embrace new learning because it helps us improve as professionals. Going back to what was mentioned in Chapter 2, we need to create the right culture and step away from our comfort zone.

Didactic Approaches: INSET days should not solely revolve around one or two people speaking at the front. This can be monotonous and restrict the representation of diverse voices in the school community. Instead, aim to incorporate various perspectives and diverse voices and expertise while ensuring that each voice is in the appropriate role to achieve the intended outcomes.

Happy Surveys and Evaluation Forms: While it is important to gather feedback on INSET days, solely relying on end-of-day participant surveys may not provide the most insightful information. Consider alternative methods for obtaining evidence of what worked well and what could be improved. Chapter 7 of the CPD evaluation can guide conducting more productive evaluations.

Overloading the Schedule: Avoid cramming too much content into INSET days, as this can overwhelm staff and leave them feeling dissatisfied. Instead, provide opportunities for staff to address their individual needs, such as setting up classrooms, having discussions with students before the official start, conducting coaching sessions, or creating informal conversations with new staff. While professional development should occur during INSET days, allow room for other important activities as well.

Pause for Thought

- Reflect on what obstacles might hinder the implementation of the suggestions mentioned earlier.
- How feasible are my suggestions, and how could they be enhanced to make your INSET days more productive?

Professional Development Sessions, Twilights, and Teachmeets

Any professional development workshops and twilight sessions scheduled for the year should concentrate on previous learning and CPD events conducted throughout the school. They should consider the daily responsibilities of teachers and evaluate the progress made since the last professional development session. This should provide an opportunity for everyone to come together and discuss the following:

- Reflect on previous commitments, and assess what has been accomplished. Remember to celebrate these small milestones.
- Engage in meaningful conversations with colleagues about various aspects of their teaching or, in the case of leadership training, leadership practices.
- Expand knowledge and thinking by connecting previous learning with new material.
- Seek feedback from others, and conceptualise the next steps (embed this into the programme schedule)

What You Should Avoid

- Viewing CPD workshops/twilight sessions as stand-alone events: By doing this, we miss the chance to fully integrate what has been learned in previous sessions. The focus should be on joined-up thinking and learning, with everything we do supporting our long-term CPD objectives and goals.

For instance, let's imagine that one of the INSET days for teachers is focused on metacognition and self-regulation, emphasising its application in the classroom, understanding how to implement this approach effectively, and the evidence supporting its significance. Based on this, you can structure your CPD workshops or twilight sessions accordingly.

The earlier suggestion serves as a framework for coordinating and sequencing twilight sessions and CPD workshops throughout the school. By implementing this approach, we can create a conducive environment and allocate sufficient time for teachers to focus on enhancing their teaching practices. Additionally, it ensures active participation from all stakeholders and provides clear guidance on the areas we are addressing.

- Allowing too much time to pass without grouping staff together to review their learning from an INSET day or CPD programme

INSET Day 1:	Twilight Session Autumn Term 1:	Twilight Session Autumn Term 1:	INSET Day 2:
Metacognition and self-regulation	Review previous learning, discuss what has been achieved, and develop learning further. Departments agree on low-stakes classroom observations to aspects of this in practice.	Teaching and learning conversations following classroom observations. Teachers should present back and use this time to seek feedback from more experienced staff and develop learning further. Additional time to be agreed on in department meetings to develop ideas further.	Review progress, and move on to your next teaching and learning focus.

can lead to a loss of momentum. Twilight sessions and CPD workshops should ideally take place within a maximum timeframe of four weeks. This ensures that the progress made during the professional development activities is effectively built upon and integrated into teachers' practice.

- Twilights/CPD workshops should not adopt a top-down approach led solely by senior leaders. It is crucial to involve everyone in the process and make it clear from the start that each individual will be able to provide input and contribute. This inclusive approach fosters collaboration, shared ownership, and a sense of empowerment among the staff.
- In the pre-COVID era, Teachmeets became prevalent in schools and regions and are highly regarded as great events. Organising such an event requires hard work (I know this only too well). They serve as fantastic celebrations of our work with students and provide an excellent platform for sharing teaching practices and pedagogy. I have personally attended several Teachmeets over the years and found them to be very helpful. However, I would like to offer a few suggestions:

- Avoid scheduling Teachmeets on Saturdays or expecting staff to attend them over the weekend. It is important not to encourage CPD activities that require teachers to invest their personal time. This approach sends a message about our school's commitment to staff well-being and work-life balance.
- Teachmeets can be valuable bite-size CPD opportunities, but more should be done to ensure their positive impact on individuals' practice. If we promote Teachmeets in our schools, it is essential to find a way to integrate the learnings from these events into the school's CPD calendar or incorporate them into conversations with coaches and mentors.
- Gather feedback from staff on what they have implemented or utilised from a Teachmeet. While the opportunity to collaborate with colleagues from other schools is invaluable, it is also important to assess which aspects of Teachmeets are working well and effectively influencing teaching practices.

Perhaps by implementing and thinking about these suggestions, we can maximise the benefits of Teachmeets and ensure they contribute meaningfully to professional development within our schools.

Pause for Thought

Does your CPD programme closely align with your larger whole-school CPD events, such as INSET days?

Do your twilight sessions and CPD workshops provide an opportunity for participants to reflect on what they have previously learned?

Online CPD

COVID has undeniably pushed us to enhance our online offering and delivery methods as facilitators and trainers. We have all become well-versed in platforms and become 'Zoom experts.' The phrase 'You're on mute' has become a common refrain in organisations and schools.

Online learning, when done effectively, serves a valuable purpose. It can be engaging through breakout rooms, polls, visuals, and interactive tools like jam boards.

What Makes a Good Online CPD Session

- A good online CPD session entails implementing clear communication and instructions prior to the session, including details on recording availability and access duration. It should feature well-structured content that flows logically, engaging delivery methods with interactive activities and participant involvement.
- As mentioned in the previous paragraph, collaborative tools like breakout rooms, chat functions, and polls should be used to foster interaction while allowing time for reflection, discussion, and questions. Follow-up resources should be provided, and feedback mechanisms should be in place to assess the effectiveness and gather participant input for continuous improvement. The session should also foster a supportive and inclusive learning environment, ensuring participant comfort and value.
- When planning sessions, clearly indicate which ones will be conducted online and which ones will be in-person training. This allows for effective communication of the session format and helps with planning. A blended approach to CPD, combining different delivery methods, works particularly well, especially for intersession activities such as bite-size PD, coaching sessions, or group meetups for review and assessment.
- Incorporate a variety of delivery styles and activities, including stepping out of presentation mode, so that the audience gets to engage with the presenter beyond slides. Encourage active participation, reflection, and questioning. Ensure diverse voices are included by choosing a range of people to share ideas and perspectives. Incorporate questions or tasks every 10 to 15 minutes to keep engagement levels high.
- Consider shorter online sessions of around 90 minutes. Longer sessions may lead to cognitive overload and disengagement, es-

pecially when conducted after school hours when participants may be tired.
- If you use an online e-learning platform with short courses, find ways to assess what colleagues have learned beyond just accepting certificates as evidence of completion. Identify any gaps in learning and provide valuable feedback.

What You Should Avoid

- Online CPD and e-learning courses do not foster collaboration among staff, as they become mere tick-box exercises without adding substantial value.
- Avoid long sessions that lack opportunities for revisiting or follow-up.
- Avoid only offering the online route. While for many of online training became necessary during COVID, relying solely on it should not be the default approach. Instead, combine face-to-face and online elements when designing CPD to create a more effective and comprehensive experience.

Educational Conferences

Educational conferences hold a special place in our hearts, and it's not just because of the delicious food! These large-scale events bring together educators from all over the world, offering a valuable opportunity for learning and the potential to forge meaningful connections. However, the effectiveness of a conference in terms of information utilisation varies greatly. Factors such as individual engagement, the relevance of the content, the quality of presentations, and the availability of follow-up support play crucial roles. While it is challenging to quantify the exact percentage of information put into use, research suggests that active participation, note-taking, reflection, and implementation strategies significantly enhance retention and application. When attending conferences, it is essential to ensure that our time and resources are utilised wisely for professional development. Instead of providing a strict list of dos and don'ts, here are some suggestions to optimise your conference experience:

- Attend a mix of sessions, including both those that are different from your usual focus and those aligned with your school's priorities. This enables you to gain fresh perspectives while engaging in meaningful discussions with colleagues.
- Set aside dedicated time in your calendar to revisit key ideas and principles from the conference. Make commitments to actionable steps, and involve others to foster accountability.
- While keynote speakers can be inspiring, take the time to reflect on how their insights can be translated into practical outcomes for you and your school. Consider how you can apply what you've learned to achieve your specific goals.
- Share your conference notes with others and establish a plan to review and reflect on them regularly. Avoid the common habit of accumulating notes without revisiting them. Actively engage with your notes to extract valuable insights, and avoid missed opportunities.

Having addressed many of the different types of CPD activities and what to look out for and avoid, let us now look at some of the logistics that ensure professional development training is effective.

Demystifying CPD Delivery: Avoiding Logistical Nightmares

Throughout my years of planning CPD sessions, I have learned the importance of gathering comprehensive information about the audience before commencing the training. This allows me to gain deeper insights into how the training aligns with the school's improvement priorities and long-term CPD objectives and ensures that I know where to pitch the content and questions put forward. One vivid incident in my memory is when I arrived at a conference to deliver workshops, only to discover at the last minute that the provided laptop had mysteriously vanished. This event required us to present using their equipment, and panic set in as we scrambled to find a replacement.

Fortunately, the session's highly interactive nature allowed me to proceed without the aid of presentation slides. Phew! Let's be honest, though, it was certainly an unwelcome surprise that could have been avoided if I had my own laptop with me as a backup. So now, wherever I go, I ensure I have my Mac and USB adaptors handy. Lesson learned: as a trainer, you must have everything covered from your end to avoid disappointment. I believe that you are only as good as your last job, so to prevent any disappointments, it's essential to be overly prepared.

To avoid such situations, here are some suggestions to consider:

Over the years, I've learned that neglecting these key factors can significantly impact the success of any CPD.

1. Always communicate your requirements well in advance. Send an introductory email outlining the necessary equipment and logistical arrangements. Look at the safeguarding example template I provided in Appendix 4. This can help clarify who will attend what sessions, when the sessions will happen, and what is expected on the day. It may be helpful to adapt it as you see fit.
   I prefer to present using my laptop, with all materials saved online. Always have an IT technician at hand; they are our saviours!
2. Clickers are invaluable tools, particularly if you move around during the session. I always bring my own to ensure smooth interaction.
3. Ensure that the room setup aligns with the content you will be presenting. There is nothing more frustrating than having activities that require participants to jot down ideas on flip chart paper, only to find that the seating arrangement doesn't support this or, worse, there is no flip chart paper available. While we teachers are adept at quickly adapting to unforeseen circumstances, it is best to prevent such situations from arising in the first place.
4. When delivering a training session in an unfamiliar location, if possible, take time to visit the room beforehand and familiarise yourself with the surroundings. This practice helps me get into the right mindset and alleviates any anxiety associated with being in an unfamiliar environment. If you are not the first speaker, it is a good idea to sit in

the room as a participant and observe the room from their point of view. This can really help you to prepare to use the space well.

While not directly related to logistics, in this era of GDPR, it is essential to ensure that everyone participating in the training session consents to share their contact details within the school. I believe sharing training resources with the audience is highly beneficial, and I encourage all facilitators to do so on the day. There may be certain elements you choose to leave out (it is our content, after all, and we've worked hard to put it together), but the more we share, the more we can learn from one another, and the more people get to hear what you are passionate about. Once again, clearly communicating these expectations before any training event is paramount, enabling your audience to understand what to anticipate.

Pause for Thought!

Is there anything else you would add to this list?

Overcoming Common Difficulties in Leading Whole-School CPD

We have all encountered situations where we find ourselves working with an audience that appears disengaged, bored, or challenging. It can be disheartening and also requires so much extra effort from us to capture their attention and involvement – the 'It won't work for me.' Participants exist in every professional development session. We know they are going to be there, so let's get prepared to change their minds.

When faced with difficult participants, it is important to consider their perspective. Perhaps what we are delivering lacks relevance to their subject areas or job roles. They may have been compelled to attend without their consent, which can understandably lead to dissatisfaction. Additionally, if it is a repeat session without follow-through or the essential components for effective professional development, their scepticism is warranted.

When faced with disengaged staff, skilled facilitators can step back and redirect the audience towards the desired outcome. This can be achieved through various approaches:

1. Adapting content and practical strategies: Flexibility is key. Don't hesitate to veer from your original plan if it means better addressing their needs.
2. Encouraging relevant questions and discussions: Actively seek their input by asking if the content is relevant to them and if it would work in their context and by inviting their agreement or disagreement.
3. Adjusting activities to suit the atmosphere: Be responsive to the climate in the room and adapt activities accordingly.
4. Ensuring active participation: Engage everyone in the session and provide positive reinforcement, even to those you may not particularly favour.

Dealing With Challenging Individuals

It is crucial to recognise that challenges from colleagues do not necessarily reflect a negative attitude. When colleagues question or challenge what is being presented, it indicates that they are actively listening and seeking to understand the relevance to their subject or their students. Cultural differences can also play a role in how information is received and interpreted.

Accepting that people's behaviour and responses may differ, it is helpful to anticipate and plan for such variations as a facilitator. Rather than perceiving challenges as confrontational, view them as an opportunity for critical thinking and constructive dialogue.

Challenges should not be viewed as inherently negative. When a colleague questions or challenges what is being presented, it signifies that they are actively engaged and seeking to understand the relevance of the content to their subject or the students they teach. It is important to recognise that cultural differences can significantly impact how information is received and interpreted. As a British Cypriot, I have observed how my own behavioural characteristics have been influenced by both the UK and Cyprus. For instance, I tend to use hand gestures frequently when explaining a point, a trait I associate with my Cypriot background. It is essential to acknowledge and accept that people's behaviours and responses can vary. As a trainer, I have often experienced different audience behaviours, and I now plan for these variations in my sessions. I encourage you to do the same, recognising and adapting to the diverse perspectives and approaches of your audience. The book 'Surrounded by Idiots' by Thomas Erikson (2019) has taught me many things and is a book I find myself going back to seek clarity on the different types of human behaviour.

So how can we effectively handle challenging situations or individuals during CPD training events? Here are some approaches to consider:

When encountering challenging individuals during a CPD training course, it is vital to approach the situation professionally and focus on productive dialogue. Here are some strategies for managing such situations:

- **Maintain a positive mindset:** Remember that challenges can provide an opportunity for growth and learning. View them as a chance to engage in constructive discussions and gain new perspectives.
- **Active listening:** Listen attentively to the concerns and opinions of the challenging person. Show respect for their viewpoint, and ensure that they feel heard and understood.
- **Empathy and understanding:** Try to empathise with their perspective and understand the underlying reasons for their challenges. Consider cultural differences, personal experiences, or any other factors that may influence their response. Bring others into the discussion. Ask what other people think, etc.
- **Rational thinking:** Respond in a calm and professional manner, even if the person becomes confrontational or disagrees strongly. Avoid becoming defensive or engaging in heated arguments.

- **Clarify and seek common ground:** Ask questions to clarify their concerns, and find areas of agreement or shared goals. Look for opportunities to build bridges, and foster mutual understanding.
- **Provide the evidence:** Support your arguments or statements with evidence, research, or real-life examples. Clearly communicate the relevance and benefits of the training content to address their concerns.
- **Address disruptive behaviour:** If the challenging behaviour becomes disruptive or disrespectful, it may be necessary to intervene and establish ground rules for maintaining a respectful and constructive learning environment. I've had to do this in the past and mentioned things that have made me feel uncomfortable after a break. For instance, addressing issues such as answering mobile phones or moving around the room without permission can help maintain focus and respect.

Remember, our goal is to create an inclusive and collaborative learning environment where everyone can benefit from the CPD training. By approaching challenging individuals with patience, understanding, and professionalism, you can navigate these situations in a productive and positive manner.

Now let's look at this in practice. What would you do in the following situations? Explore these three scenarios, and jot down how you would manage each individual.

Scenario 1

Teacher A, a veteran teacher with strong opinions, tends to dominate discussions during training sessions. They often interrupt others, dismiss alternative viewpoints, and monopolise the conversation.

Scenario 2

Teacher B, a new teacher, is often disengaged and unresponsive during training sessions. They appear disinterested, rarely participate in activities or discussions, and seem reluctant to contribute.

Scenario 3

Teacher C, who is highly critical and resistant to change, often challenges the validity or applicability of new concepts or strategies introduced during training sessions. They may express scepticism, offer counterarguments, or dismiss ideas without giving them a fair chance.

Let's explore some possible approaches for effectively dealing with these three participants. Take a moment to review these suggestions and consider your agreement with them. It's important to note that these approaches are not absolute or exhaustive but provide a perspective on handling such situations.

Scenario 1: Teacher A

- Acknowledge Teacher A's contributions but emphasise the importance of creating space for everyone to share their perspectives.
- Encourage turn-taking and redirect questions to other participants.
- Provide opportunities for small group discussions to ensure diverse voices are heard.

Scenario 2: Teacher B

- Create a safe and inclusive environment where Teacher B feels comfortable sharing their thoughts.
- Use active learning techniques like group activities or hands-on exercises to encourage participation.
- Provide specific prompts or questions directly relating to Teacher B's interests or teaching context.

Scenario 3: Teacher C

- Acknowledge Teacher C's concerns and validate their perspective.
- Provide evidence, examples, or case studies that support the effectiveness of the concepts being discussed.
- Invite Teacher C to share their experiences or propose alternative

solutions, fostering constructive dialogue.

Conclusion

This chapter has explored the essential principles to consider when designing and delivering effective professional development. We discussed the practical frameworks I (and you can) follow when planning CPD and expanded on ideas and research evidence from previous chapters. Use this chapter as a how-to guide when planning your CPD activities and training events, such as CPD programmes, INSET days, and twilights. It's important to remember that good teachers need to be developed, and to ensure excellent professional development, we must take these considerations into account. By incorporating these elements, we can reap the benefits of effective professional development that supports professional growth in knowledge and practice. If you are reading this as a CPD leader or someone responsible for leading teaching and learning in your school, you've now gained vital insight into things you should consider when planning your professional development. You know what you need to do to prepare to deliver CPD. You will ensure you consider all of the logistics and, of course, the participants themselves. Implementing many of the strategies I've outlined will enhance the overall experience and standard of continuing professional development (CPD) in our schools. Implementing some of the strategies I've mentioned may just enrich the experience and quality of CPD in our schools as well as capitalise on the 'C' of professional development, creating a common thread across everything that we do.

Reflective Questions

1. To what extent does the professional development in your school effectively align across each programme? How do you ensure that staff members are well-informed about this alignment?
2. How do you ensure your CPD training sessions encompass all the necessary elements?

How to Plan and Deliver Effective Teacher CPD 107

3. Do you adhere to a specific framework or theoretical structure when planning and delivering CPD sessions?
4. What additional factors would you include in each section of 'what to avoid' to ensure that potential pitfalls are addressed?
5. If you were to summarise this chapter in one paragraph, what key insights or main takeaways would you highlight?
6. How do you incorporate Kolb's reflective cycle into your school's CPD schedule or training sessions?
7. When preparing to deliver CPD, what actions do you take in advance to ensure that all logistical aspects are thoroughly addressed and the training session is set up for success?
8. What measures can be taken to incorporate appropriate challenges during CPD delivery?
9. How do you handle disengaged participants, and which of the suggestions provided might you consider implementing?
10. Do you prepare for difficult questions when delivering CPD?
11. What questions or areas of further exploration has this chapter raised for you?
12. What aspects of this chapter resonated with you the most, and why?

Chapter Snapshots

- Planning excellent CPD involves relevance to school needs, up-to-date content, seamless delivery, assessment, reflection, and follow-up plans. No one should leave your session not knowing what to do.
- It's important to understand your audience, and engaging them before CPD training is important. Clearly define the short-term and long-term learning outcomes from the start and where we might be going.
- Plan CPD with follow-up activities in mind to ensure knowledge and strategies are effectively integrated.
- CPD should aim to provide new knowledge and promote progress

in thinking and practice – and not just make colleagues feel inspired.
- Successful professional development relies on well-sequenced and interconnected activities, allowing participant choice.
- When delivering professional development, encourage interactive teaching methods over didactic ones. Professional development should be about more than just an audience listening to one or two people.
- Effective presentation skills are essential, but participant engagement is even more critical.
- Consider Kolb's (2015) reflective learning theory, which involves concrete experience, reflective observation, abstract conceptualisation, and active experimentation in professional development planning.
- Explore the great teaching model for effective teaching, and apply a similar approach to your school's CPD planning/CPD programme schedule.
- We plan different types of professional development opportunities for colleagues in our schools, including CPD programmes, INSET days, conferences, twilight sessions, online sessions, etc. Planning differs for each, so referring to the dos and don'ts can be a useful checklist
- When leading whole-school CPD, ensure representation from every department or faculty in your material.
- A challenging teacher during a CPD session is not necessarily a negative; it can be constructive to turn scepticism into a positive force. Use the guidance given such as listening with empathy and providing good evidence to support the case. However, at the same time, it is essential to address and not tolerate rudeness or unprofessional behaviour as necessary.

References

Coe, R. et al.(2020) *Great teaching toolkit: Evidence review*. Evidence-Based Education & Cambridge Assessment International Education. Available at: https://f.hubspotusercontent30.net/hubfs/2366135/Great%20Teaching%20Toolkit%20Evidence%20Review.pdf.

Erikson, T. (2019) *Surrounded by idiots: The four types of human behaviour (or, how to understand those who cannot be understood)*. Translated by M. Pender and R. Bradbury. London: Vermilion.

Guskey, T. R. (2002). Professional development and teacher change. *Teachers and Teaching: Theory and Practice*, 8(3/4), 381-391.

Kolb, D.A. (2015) *Experiential learning: Experience as the source of learning and development*. 2nd edition. Upper Saddle River, NJ: Pearson Education, Inc.

Lemov, D. (2021) *Teach like a champion 3.0:63 techniques that put students on the path to college*. 3rd edition. Hoboken, NJ: Jossey-Bass, a Wiley Imprint.

Rosenshine, B. (2012) 'Principles of instruction: Research-based strategies that all teachers should know', *American Educator*, Spring, pp. 12–39.

6 Enhancing CPD Through Effective Coaching

Coaching can be one of the most powerful methods of teacher development that I have witnessed. It helps teachers and school leaders develop the skill sets they need to improve their schools' outcomes. All teachers want to improve, and coaching helps them to do just that. When it isn't, it soon becomes just another buzzword floating around our schools. The purpose of this chapter is not necessarily to provide different types of coaching (such as executive coaching, leadership, peer coaching, and so on – there's already a wealth of helpful information on this on the World Wide Web). Instead, I'd like to focus on how coaching can effectively change teachers' attitudes and behaviours by fostering collaborations among more experienced peers and embedding coaching into our professional development programmes to help achieve long-term aims and objectives. However, I have included a section on incremental and instructional coaching because I believe it can be handy for school leaders aiming to enhance the quality of lesson observation feedback. It has been helpful for me, and I'd like to share my perspective on how this can be done.

In this chapter, we will cover the following:

- Review the fundamental principles of coaching and effective communication.
- Explore the foundational aspects of coaching that need to be present across our schools for it to work and be successful.
- Instructional coaching to help teachers develop.

What is coaching?

Coaching is a process that can happen between peers. It is a collaborative process of improving specific skills. Coach and coachee meet on mutual ground to set goals and provide space to discuss, plan, and reflect upon the pathway towards meeting those goals. Although the coach may have more experience than the coachee, they use their experience to support, question, and guide their charge towards success. This process is nondirective and empowering.

How is coaching different from mentoring?

A mentor will have more experience than their mentee. The mentor will set goals and often use their experience to tell their charge how to meet those goals. This is a directive process, led by the mentor, to improve the mentee's skills and understanding through their own lived experiences.

Coaching should not be viewed as a replacement for mentoring; both coaching and mentoring have unique roles to fulfil in our schools.

So coaching is a collaborative experience between peers. There is a lot of evidence available to us which shows the positive impact of teacher collaboration. One such investigation comes from Andy Hargreaves and Michael Fullan, 'Professional Capital, Transforming Teaching in Every School' (2012). Teachers learn more when they can work, plan, and talk about teaching and learning. Coaching (and mentoring) can play a significant part in this process, enabling teachers to work together to engage in professional dialogue.

Exploring Principles and Practices

Coaching has its roots in psychotherapy and counselling. However, the way that coaching is applied in a professional setting is often different. Professional coaching, like counselling, focuses on helping people and using similar interpersonal communication skills. Although both are intended to enable people to achieve their full potential, their roles differ. Coaching is used professionally to enable someone to realise their potential by focusing on the future and reflecting on situations that arise at work. Counselling is used for personal reasons, and one often looks at the past to uncover what might have led to this issue.

Here are several ways that coaching has been described in a professional setting.

Coaching involves unlocking a person's potential to maximise their performance. It's about helping them learn rather than teaching them.

John Whitmore (2017)

Coaching is the art of facilitating the performance, learning and development of another.

Myles Downey (2003)

Coaching is helping move ones thinking forward to find new solutions by asking powerful questions.

Jackie Beere (2016)

Coaching is the art of facilitating another person's learning, development and performance. Through coaching, people are able to find their own solutions develop their own skills and their own behaviours and attitudes.

Viv Grant (2014)

Which of the earlier descriptions would best fit your school's philosophy?

Coaching means different things to different people, which is okay as long as everyone involved is absolutely clear on your school's definition. If you are going to invest in embedding coaching, you need to have a clear definition of what coaching means to your school community. You need to know how coaching will be used to support practitioners moving forward in their teaching, leadership, or pastoral roles. Everyone should be fully committed, and coaching should not be offered to anyone who does not want it.

Once, many moons ago, I was asked to coach a member of staff who was underperforming. My headteacher thought it would benefit them, as I had quite a good relationship with this person. While the intention was good, the message sent to that staff member could have been better. Coaching, in this instance, was being used to intervene in underperformance. The process wasn't initiated by the person; they saw me as a threat, and the message to them was that they were not good enough. They politely and rightly declined to be coached despite our good relationship. Coaching should not be seen as a last resort. It should not be forced upon them. It should be an integral part of our whole-school practice.

Coaching, as a form of professional development, works because it offers personalised support, encourages reflective practice, promotes skill development, and fosters a growth mindset. The view that leaders take of coaching has evolved since my experience earlier. We no longer associate underperforming colleagues with coaching, and many CPD programmes include coaching as part of their ongoing training cycle.

Coaching Works Well in the Following Situations:

- We are focused on building trusted, confidential relationships. The golden principles are visible, and this language is used across the school.
- The right people become coaches in schools, especially when we are looking at using instructional/incremental coaching to improve teaching in our schools.
- It gives teachers time to grow and develop.
- This is embedded in ongoing teacher CPD programmes/in-house INSETs and twilights.

Coaching Will Not Work in the Following Situations:

- It is implemented as a tick-box intervention (nothing that ticks a box makes any real difference, and coaching is no different).
- Not enough training is given to coaches to develop their coaching skills.
- Schools have a summative system for assessing the effectiveness of their staff.
- Coaches and coachees do not have time to meet during the school day. The coach must be given a reduced teaching load for coaching sessions to be meaningful and effective. If arranging internal coaching in your school/trust proves tricky, bring-

ing in external coaches may be a better option. This allows the coaching to be done effectively and for its value to be fully understood.

Who Should Coach?

We must carefully choose the individuals to take on coaching roles within our schools. Coaches should not simply be chosen because they are long-serving teachers who have achieved outstanding results nor should they be the person's line manager. A coach must possess specific qualities and skills to excel in this role. They must be proficient in active listening and able to absorb information effectively. Reflecting accurately on a problem or situation is crucial.

Additionally, they should excel in the art of questioning, capable of exploring and supporting with precision. Effective communication skills are a must, allowing coaches to provide feedback that propels their coachees forward. These are just a few of the essential human skills required to be a high-quality coach.

It's important to note that not all teachers, including middle and senior leaders, naturally possess these skills. Therefore, coaches must receive the necessary training and support to excel in this role. It's crucial, at this point, to emphasise that, like any school intervention, our success hinges on having the right resources and tools in place from the start. In recent years, I have observed coaching being applied loosely in schools, often without a deep understanding of when and how it should be used. If you are reading this thinking this is happening in my schools, take some time to think about what you would change.

Transactional Analysis and Coaching

I first came across transactional analysis (TA) as part of my psychology degree at university. In his 1964 book, 'Games People Play: The Psychology of Human Relationships', Eric Berne uses the concept of ego states to explain human behaviour. Bernes believes that when we communicate, we do so through using one of three ego states, which include the following:

Parent: authoritarian, disciplinarian, loving, nurturing
Child: co-operative, spontaneous, rebellious, needy, creative
Adult: rational, logical, respectful, controlling our emotions

We are not fixed to one state. Different people bring out different aspects of our personality. For example, when I am with my childhood friends (as much as we try to have mature conversations), we regress back to being 14. This is perfectly normal. We regress to our child state with each other. Bernes states that, for effective communication to happen, the people communicating must be in the same ego state as each other. For my friends and I, our shared ego state is comfortable and allows us to communicate with ease. However, the same ego state is not always easy to gain or maintain.

In a professional capacity, when we are dealing with challenging behaviour, for example, a colleague who has been unprofessional or challenging, we may find that the person we are communicating with is presenting to us a child's ego. When this occurs, we should always aim to remain in the adult ego state to ensure that our conversation is as effective as possible. The adult is rational and respectful. They listen to facts over emotions and can use this to reach a sensible conclusion. If we were to match the child's ego in a challenging professional situation, the rebel in us both may not allow an effective conclusion to the discussion, and it may spiral into chaos. Similarly, the parent's ego may dominate the child and control the situation but is unlikely to reach the positive conclusion that the adult would.

When applying transactional analysis theory, we can better control and regulate our behaviours by recognising our egoic state at any given time. As coaches, we aim to be in the adult ego state. This enables us to ask good questions, with the ability to pause and reflect, which positively impacts our capacity to communicate effectively. When coaching colleagues and delving into sensitive and personal experiences, there will be moments when the coachee's emotional state may change. By applying transactional analysis theory, the coach can remain present, regulate themselves, and work towards the most effective conclusion for the situation.

Teacher Collaboration

The coaching process naturally fits into a school that thrives on collaboration. A coaching conversation feels organic when teachers are accustomed to discussing, evaluating, and sharing their practices. It doesn't come across as imposed upon them, and it is more likely to involve a constructive exchange between two adults without ego conflicts.

As I mentioned in Chapter 4, we need to create school systems and procedures that enable teachers to keep learning and reflecting on their teaching. Building atomic habits (where we make our bad habits invisible and our good habits showcased from the rooftops) is where we need to be. In his book 'The Jigsaw of a Successful School,' Sir Tim Brighouse (2006) refers to the work of American researcher Judith Little. Sir Tim talks about several ways the following four aspects create a culture of teaching and learning. This includes the following:

- Teachers talk about teaching.
- Teachers observe each other and teach.
- Teachers plan, organise, monitor, and evaluate their teaching together.
- Teachers teach each other.

The most successful schools are those where teaching and learning are the core business, where every system is in place to ensure that teaching and learning can be of high quality.

Pause for Reflection

Take some time to think about your school. Read each of the following questions to help you explore your school's current practice.

- When and how often do teachers have the chance to talk about their teaching or to observe each other teach?
- What happens after an observation?
- When do teachers have the chance to teach other colleagues across their schools and faculties?
- How do we create opportunities to share information?

Enhancing CPD Through Effective Coaching

We can instruct teachers to implement new practices. Still, our efforts will remain superficial if we fail to provide the necessary support. Teachers should have ample opportunities to collaborate as educators. For teachers to gain confidence and effectively enhance their teaching, I believe the following should be in place:

- **Collaborative Choice:** Teachers should be able to focus on their strengths and areas they've identified for improvement, enabling them to enhance their teaching continually. By concentrating on their strengths, they can amplify their successes. Also, allowing individuals to choose their best practices for collaboration with others can serve as a strong motivator for further improvement.
- **Collaborative Alignment:** Everyone should be on the same page, and we need to establish from the onset what specific goals we hope to achieve. Although things may change organically, everyone working together must know why we are doing this, how we will do it, and what we will do.
- **Collaborative Accountability:** Teachers (and everyone involved) in supporting an individual's progress should be held responsible for their commitments, actions, and the reasons behind them. At the same time, as senior leaders, we must ensure the right resources to support their efforts for any collaboration to succeed and for us to hold people accountable. If any barriers exist, we need to identify them and address how we can overcome them. We are still accountable for regularly checking in to assess its effectiveness and ensure the intended impact is seen. When there's a sense of collective responsibility, it motivates everyone to work together towards achieving the desired outcomes.
- **Collaborative Support:** Whilst all the aforementioned are essential, none of the aforementioned will work without the support of peers and colleagues. Supporting such quality time to facilitate teaching and learning conversations and coaching will make the chance of change more successful.

Coaching for Effective CPD

Coaching should be effectively integrated into your school's holistic professional development plan rather than existing in isolation. When executed successfully, this integration will reveal the true impact of coaching in supporting professional growth and teachers in the classroom. Teachers will recognise the connections between INSET days and coaching, observations and coaching, and performance management and coaching. It should all be seamlessly woven into the larger whole-school vision for success.

Historically, there have been two distinct approaches guiding educational improvement:

> **The Pedagogical Approach:** In this approach, individuals become experts through reading, taking tests, passing exams, and entering the workforce to apply the acquired knowledge and skills. Here, professionals are responsible for managing their professional growth.
>
> **The Developmental Approach:** Rooted in coaching, this approach emphasises that learning is a continuous process and individuals are never a finished product. Originally derived from sports, it revolves around the principle that coaches support athletes to enhance specific aspects of their expertise. Coaches provide feedback, and with guided support, athletes refine their skills over time.

The developmental approach is now favoured over the pedagogical approach across most Western countries. A developmental approach is a coaching approach. Leaving practitioners to work in isolation simply doesn't work. Coaching systems in our school are the best way to reach our goals effectively. However, there are plenty of other ways for teachers to collaborate with their colleagues. Refer to Table 6.1 for a variety of collaborative opportunities commonly seen in schools. While not exhaustive, this list reflects my teaching experience and things I have implemented in my schools. Feel free to add your own examples and use this as a brief activity to assess the benefits with your colleagues. By doing this, you can reflect on your current practices and identify opportunities for fostering a more collaborative culture in your school

Table 6.1 Sharing Good Practice: Exploring Types of Teacher Collaborations in Schools

Types of Teacher Collaborations	Yes/No	Frequency	By Who?	What's Working Well?	What could We Improve?
Coaching, e.g. executive coaching, instructional coaching, peer coaching.					
Mentoring					
Work shadowing					
Team teaching					
Teaching and learning communities					
A cycle of peer observations/ feedback meetings that all teachers complete as part of the professional development					
Time to talk meetings (no pens, no paper, just talking about great teaching)					
Regional network events					
Lesson planning (expert teachers paired up with novice teachers).					

Although some of the aforementioned might be more feasible to adopt than others on a scale of 1–10 (10 being highly successful in my school and 1 being not in place at all), where would you place each of the CPD opportunities on this scale? Are we fully embracing the research we have available to us in this area and making this visible in our schools? This is a helpful activity we can try out with our senior and middle leaders, which will help us evaluate where we might be in providing teachers with an opportunity to work and learn from other colleagues.

To ensure the effectiveness of coaching, several key factors must be in place:

- **Excellent Training:** Providing comprehensive training to develop highly skilled coaches is crucial. Not cutting corners here is essential, as coaching is demanding work. Coaches should receive proper training and supervision to enhance their skill set and support their well-being. Attending a short one or two-day coaching course may only equip them with some of the necessary tools for successful coaching.
- **Allocated Time:** Coaches should have dedicated time during the school day for coaching sessions. No one should be expected to meet outside of their regular working hours.
- **Alignment with School Culture:** Coaching should align with the school's culture and performance development model. It should focus on more than summative data for assessing teaching quality.
- **Timetable and Scheduling:** A coaching timetable with clear dates and times should be established to ensure everyone involved understands the commitments and to avoid conflicts with other work responsibilities.
- **Trust and Confidentiality:** Building trust and maintaining confidentiality is paramount. All stakeholders, including coaches and coachees, should feel confident that what is shared during coaching sessions remains confidential. Coaches should be selected with no hidden agendas, ensuring judgments do not reach senior managers, which can compromise the coaching process.

Fostering Strong Coaching Relationships – My Five Golden Principles

All coaching relationships are built on what I call the five golden principles. Coaches should ensure that these are in place if they are to have successful learning conversations. I've adapted my five principles from Jim Knight's 'The Definitive Guide to Instructional Coaching' (2021). They provide a helpful framework for building a successful relationship between a coach and their coachee.

- **Egalitarianism:** Both the coach and the coachee are equal. There is no hierarchy in place, and the individual being coached must not feel inferior to the coach. Conversations need to be rooted in trust, hope, and humility without judgment.
- **Co-operation:** Learning is a two-way street; when coaching is grounded in co-operation, coaches and teachers learn together. The coach must ensure that they remain impartial and non-judgmental through their questioning, and coaches value the ideas teachers share with them.
- **Autonomy:** Coaches should aim to create relationships that encourage choice – conversations where the coachee decides on change. Coaches should show they are listening through good questioning and provide the language of choice to empower and show that the teachers' opinions matter.
- **Reflection:** Coaches should act in a way that encourages the art of purposeful reflection. We are trying wherever possible to 'pull' rather than to 'push' others to think for themselves by asking great questions. Reflective conversations should focus on looking back at what's been done, providing evidence, reviewing effectiveness, applying modifications, and looking ahead to what we will do.
- **Praxis:** Derived from the Greek word for putting an idea into practice, praxis is a crucial coaching component. Learning between a coach/coachee must be grounded in someone's reality. Conversations should be relevant, and learning will only be successful if learning encompasses their experiences and what is important to them. Only then will the ideas be put into practice 'praxis.'

By considering these five principles, we can establish a framework for building successful coaching relationships and define the role of coaching within our schools. These principles not only help structure coaching conversations but also remind us of the ethical considerations that must be upheld when using coaching as a tool for professional growth.

Questioning for Personal Growth

Effective questioning for coaches is an art that goes hand in hand with active listening. As Stephen Covey aptly puts it, listening to understand before seeking to be understood is crucial in collaboration. However, it's not as easy as it sounds. It's easy to become distracted by other thoughts, such as upcoming meetings or pending tasks like grading exercise books. The real power of effective coaching lies in the ability to ask the right questions. To achieve this, we must remain fully present in the moment with our coachee. Distractions can significantly hinder our listening and questioning abilities.

Types of Questions

I highly recommend reading 'Coaching for Performance – The Principles and Practice for Effective Coaching and Leadership (5th Edition)' by Sir John Whitmore (2017) and 'Coaching Conversations: Transforming Your School One Conversation at a Time' by Linda M. Gross Cheliotes and Marceta F. Reilly (2010). These books provide valuable insights and guidance for those looking to enhance their coaching knowledge and skills.

While having a bank of questions can be helpful, it's crucial to note that there should be no scripted approach in coaching sessions. Good intuition is often more important than any predefined set of questions. Coaches serve as awareness raisers, achieving this by asking insightful questions that encourage deep thinking and critical reflection. They avoid suggestive questions that might divert coachees from their thought processes. Coaches excel at using questions that are as follows:

- Empowering
- Build curiosity
- Non-judgmental
- Non-critical
- Respectful
- Unscripted
- Understand when to use open/closed questions

- Language of choice
- Foster a growth mindset
- Fuelled by listening
- Reflective on the past, moment and future

The GROW model of coaching is a great starting point for structuring and guiding impactful coaching conversations. This model has been refined since its initial development by Graham Alexander, Alan Fine, and Sir John Whitmore in the 1980s. The four letters of the acronym spell out a simple yet effective framework for helping individuals achieve their goals:

- Goal setting (What do you want to achieve?)
- Reality (What's this really like?)
- Option evaluation (or obstacle identification)
- Way forward (What will you do?)

In each phase, the coach's questions will support the coachee to move towards success. If you want to learn more about this powerful model and how to use it effectively, you can download a set of coaching questions I created for Veema Education from their website.

https://veema.co.uk/news-media/#NEWSANDINSIGHTS

If you are new to coaching, consider practising your questioning skills with other coaches until you are comfortable using this approach independently.

Reflection on Coaching Questions

Use the following table to explore question types further. Ask yourself when the most appropriate times during a coaching session are to use each question type. What might the effect be of choosing the wrong type of question, and why?

Effective Questioning Is Rooted in Attentive Listening

To listen effectively, it's essential to maintain control over our own thoughts and stay focused. This involves paying close attention to

Table 6.2 Reflecting on Coaching Questions

Type of Questions	Example Questions	Its Effect
Closed	• On a scale of 1–5, how easy could you implement this strategy? • Will this teaching strategy work with this class?	At the start and end of your conversation. It helps structure the conversations and next steps.
Open	• What will help you implement this teaching strategy? • What could you do to ensure you will implement this strategy effectively?	Offer guided practice when modelling and talking through steps.
Reflective	• Why do you think this worked well when you implemented this strategy? • If you were to try this strategy again, what would you do definitely?	Focuses the conversations on looking back, looking at, and looking forward.
Understanding self	• What do you think this means in reality? • How does this help you and your students?	Encourages deeper thinking and exploration of a practitioner's teaching practice.
Developer	• Let's look at this together a little more. • How did you do that?	Unravel more detail and new ideas for deeper probing.
Clarifying	• Have I understood this correctly? • What do you mean by this? Explain this to me again so I make sure I've understood it correctly.	Avoid misunderstandings and misconceptions.
Feedback	• What would you do with this feedback? • How will you seek feedback to know whether this has worked or not?	Opportunity to set actional next steps and reconvey the strategy for successful implementation.
Directive questions	• Let's practice this strategy together. • What worked well when you tried this approach with your class/this student?	When refocusing the conversation.

verbal and non-verbal communication during a coaching session. By doing so, we strengthen the conversation and convey to our colleagues that we are fully engaged, managing our internal thought processes while remaining attuned to external cues visible to others.

This understanding of how to demonstrate active listening and its significance is crucial.

Pay Attention to Both Verbal and Non-Verbal Forms of Communication

Not only what is verbally expressed during a coaching session requires effective questioning. A good coach will look for non-verbal cues that may be a sign of how someone is feeling. Looking away or folding our arms may reveal something that requires us to go a little deeper. Additionally, tone of voice may reveal that something is not quite right or working very well.

Note-Taking

Taking notes can be a helpful tool for showing that you are listening to what is being said. You can come back to what has been previously discussed to add more meaning to the conversation and show the other person that you are listening to what is important to them. Be careful to explain why you need to take notes from the start and how these will remain confidential. If the other person would like copies of this, it is best practice to send them after each session with the clear actions that have been agreed upon.

Ask for Clarification

Asking someone to recap or clarify their points and thinking further shows that you are listening and controls your thinking to hear your conversation partner better.

Environment

Choose a space that prevents you from getting caught up in other school matters. We will struggle to have coaching sessions if we organise them in our offices or in other open spaces where others can easily interrupt our flow. Choose a private space away from the hustle and bustle of school life. You need a space that not only creates the psychological safety of creating trust and builds confidentiality but that also enables you to give your full attention as a coach to your coachee.

For effective listening and questioning, I would suggest you consider most of the following:

- Prioritise having your conversation partner do the majority of the talking.
- Take pauses to acknowledge and reflect before contributing your thoughts.
- Minimise interruptions, and do this only when absolutely necessary.
- Present one question at a time for better clarity and understanding.
- Request clarification when unsure.
- Include the question 'And what else?' to encourage further discussions.
- Steer clear of posing leading questions.

Instructional Coaching

As we now know, instructional coaching often differs from traditional coaching models, as it takes a more directive than non-directive approach. Many of us first became aware of this approach in 'Leverage Leadership' by Paul Bambrick-Santoyo and Lemov (2018) and 'The Definitive Guide to Instructional Coaching' by John Knight (2021). This type of coaching focuses exclusively on teaching and learning and includes explaining and modelling from a more experienced teacher.

In an instructional coaching relationship, the coach requires expert teaching knowledge to provide helpful feedback and guidance that pushes the coachee teacher beyond their comfort zone. While the coach acts as the expert, they work in partnership in a supportive role, facilitating their coachee teacher through questioning to set targets and identify the strategy and action steps.

As mentioned earlier, collaborative partnership is crucial, and for it to thrive, it is essential not to impose goals on teachers, even if we know them well. Instead, teachers should autonomously establish their goals, aligning them with desired student outcomes and grounded in a realistic assessment of their classroom practices. When working in tandem as a coach, your role involves presenting this information.

Examples of teacher goals:

- Enhancing teaching practices for a new scheme of work scheme, particularly when teaching it for the first time.
- Providing stretch and challenge for SEND pupils to ensure ongoing progress.
- Improving assessment techniques to deliver timely and constructive feedback to pupils.
- Integrating technology to elevate student engagement and enhance learning outcomes.

One of the remarkable aspects of instructional coaching is its transformation of lesson observations. Traditional observations have often been non-developmental, high-stakes, and stressful for teachers, failing to provide effective feedback and support for improvement. Instructional coaching redefines lesson observations, making them meaningful and empowering for teachers, offering guided support to implement and embed teaching strategies effectively.

Instructional coaching primarily relies on guided questioning to help coachees achieve their goals. The teaching and learning coach partners with the teacher in these conversations exclusively focused on teaching and learning. The coachee retains control over how they reach their desired outcomes.

Instructional coaching also involves deliberate practice. The coaching sessions identify a narrow focus, leading to intensive practice with high-quality feedback, excellent explanations, and modelling of teaching practices until the goal is met. The continuous reviews of practice fine-tune teaching strategies as needed. Instructional coaching focuses on practical learning dialogue but includes modelling, guided practice, and step-by-step support from an expert teaching and learning practitioner.

Instructional coaching has gathered the attention of school leaders as a powerful intervention to help teachers improve in the classroom. It includes all the right ingredients for teachers to identify, learn, practice, and re-evaluate their classroom teaching. I'm a fan, but at the same time, I'm a realist. We must carefully consider how practical it is for all schools to implement instructional coaching if teaching and learning lead practitioners have heavy teaching timetables. This would restrict them from carrying out this role correctly. However, if we are brave and allocate the appropriate amount of time to this role, the process would lead to outstanding practices in our schools. How much are we willing to invest?

Over the past three to five years, I have integrated instructional coaching into my professional development programmes because I truly see the benefits of this type of collaborative coaching in enhancing teachers' classroom practice and knowledge of pedagogy. However, for it to be effective, I encourage you to incorporate as many of the following suggestions.

- Instructional coaching is a long-term investment. Coaches/coachees work together over a 12-18-month period.
- Instructional coaches are excellent classroom practitioners and earn this respect from colleagues.
- Instructional coaches must be able to explain and model good teaching practices to ensure the coachee meets their goal.
- An instructional coach should be independent of line-managing their coachee.
- Instructional coaches must facilitate good teaching and learning questions, provide prompts and clues if the teacher is stuck, and scaffold and model teaching techniques for successful implementation.
- Instructional coaching involves a short, non-judgmental lesson observation followed by action-based coaching. Coaching sessions should happen on the same day as the observation.
- Instructional coaches must provide in-class support – team teaching, facilitating peer observations, lesson walkthroughs, etc.
- Instructional coaches must cultivate a 'collaborative' partnership, encouraging teachers to determine which aspects of their teaching practice to improve.
- Instructional coaches should teach the same or fewer hours as your senior leaders.
- Instructional coaches should meet with coachee teachers during the school day.

Pause for Reflection

> What should my approach to coaching be to support teacher development and improve classroom practices effectively?

Like the GROW model I mentioned earlier, when I use instructional coaching in schools, I refer to Jim Knight's 'Impact Cycle.' This cycle consists of three key elements: identify, learn, and improve. This cycle is a powerful process to help teachers decide on their areas of development and meet them. I'll briefly touch upon each stage later.

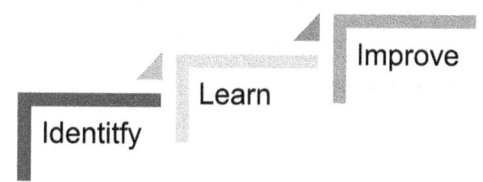

A model adapted from Jim Knight's 2018 work, 'The Impact Cycle: What Instructional Coaches Should Do to Foster Powerful Improvements in Teaching.'

Stage 1: Identity

For instructional coaching to succeed, the first stage must include identifying with your coachee where they currently are and where they hope to be in the future. Teachers reflect on what good teaching and pedagogy look like within given frameworks. For the coachee to have autonomy and ownership over this journey and for accurate goals to be agreed upon, we must establish the teacher's reality.

This can be done by doing the following:

- Arranging an initial pre-coaching meeting to get to know your collaborating teacher.
- Discussing high-quality teaching within the broader context – referencing key frameworks for concrete evidence. The literature referenced in Chapters 2, 3, and 4 should be helpful here.
- Determining a clear picture of 'reality' for the teacher before setting their goals and reflecting on good teaching. This can be done by observing the teacher's lesson or video footage of a lesson, in-

terviewing students, and reviewing students' work and test scores.
- Identifying a student-centred goal by working with their coach based on data. You may choose to use PEERS goals (powerful, easy, emotionally compelling, reachable, and student-focused), which prompt the teacher to think about setting goals that are meaningful to them.
- Reviewing data and evidence assists teachers in pinpointing the areas they should concentrate on. Encourage teachers to reflect on and define meaningful aspects of their practice, helping them establish systems to attain these desired outcomes.
- Identifying the strategies and pathways teachers will take. Setting the path for how you are going to meet the goal. This, for me, is even more important than the goal itself.

Stage 2: Learn

Now that the coachee knows their starting point through the coach's assistance, the magic of learning begins. I love this cycle stage, as it enables you to bring the strategy to life and build effective habits to keep everything alive (remember how important atomic habits are for performance). The coach's job is to ensure the coachee teacher can use the strategy identified in stage 1 of the cycle.

This can be done by doing the following:

- Explaining and modelling the strategies one at a time. Reinforce this through a simple checklist or steps that someone can take. I love checklists, as they really help me provide concrete steps on how you can achieve your desired outcomes to ensure everything is in place.
- Asking good questions to develop teachers' thinking so that you are confident they have understood how to use the teaching techniques.
- Modelling the strategies in the classroom. This is the most important part of step 2. This happens by modelling in the classroom, showing a video of strategies, team teaching, peer observations, or watching another person's lesson. You can use a simple checklist to model the key steps and features of the method.

Pause for Reflection

> To what degree does modelling play a role in your coaching approach in your school?

Stage 3: Improve

This stage is about implementing the strategy. The 'doing' part is putting pedagogy and your learning into action. During this stage, the coach and coachee must review the goal and explore its success by reviewing data gathered through lesson observations or on video and adjusting until the goal is met.

This can be done by doing the following:

- Recapping the direction and goals set during step 1.
- Ensuring meetings are focused on reviewing the progress that directly links to student progress.
- Whether the strategy is working. Making sense of what it means to genuinely improve over time and determining whether the teacher has an understanding of whether they have met the goal and the impact of deep and surface learning is essential.
- Using a lesson observation template. (I've included an example of a coaching lesson observation template in Appendix 3 for your reference and adaptation in your work.) You can use or adapt this template to suit what's best for your coaches and school. The most important thing to remember here is that note-taking refers to what will be discussed following the coaching observation to help evaluate the success of the teaching strategy. Anything written down on this template must be confidential and shared with the coachee.
- If you are using video, I recommend that the coach/teachers watch this separately before their meeting. Video footage can focus on students during the lesson and not necessarily on the teacher. This is a powerful method to capture what students are learning and doing at the moment, which can facilitate great coaching conversations.
- Coach/teacher needs to agree on the next action steps until the

participating teacher achieves the goal.

The Impact Cycle is a very useful framework that can help us embed instructional coaching in our schools. Based on the aforementioned, what questions do you have about the Impact Cycle? Is approaching teacher coaching in this way a useful tool for improving a teacher's classroom practice? I believe it is, but at the same time, we need to truly understand how to embed such an approach in our schools and whether this aligns with our principles for improving high-quality teachers. Starting with simplicity is wise if you're new to instructional coaching or have limited resources. You can focus lesson observations on the fundamental principles of instructional coaching and use this approach to enhance the feedback and support more experienced practitioners in providing teachers. Keep it simple, and you can start with the following cycle with a handful of teachers.

Step 1: Coach observes a lesson or reviews a video.
Step 2: Brief coaching session on the same day.
Step 3: Collaboratively set a goal and strategy with your coachee, then explain and model the steps for successful implementation.
Step 4: The teacher spends up to two weeks practising.
Step 5: Coach and coachee review the impact and make improvements to meet the goal.

Meaningful Lesson Observations

The best schools allow teachers to learn from their mistakes and try new things. Lesson observations can be an excellent learning tool, encouraging us to evaluate and solve problems. I have yet to meet any school leader who doesn't want to improve the way lesson observations are conducted, ensuring consistency across all departments and faculties across the school. Let's be honest; ensuring everything and everyone works in alignment in our school is hard work. When done well and with thoughtful consideration, lesson observations can facilitate meaningful teaching and learning conversations, especially when these are carried out by colleagues who are recognised and respected as being excellent teachers.

In Appendix 5, I have included a template that I find particularly helpful for conducting targeted, focused observations that support teachers in improving an area of their teaching. I like using a simple resource like this because it demonstrates how the observer, at the time of the observation, is working with the observee to provide practical and meaningful support after the observation by recording key aspects that will form the feedback conversation. The template allows you to record the teaching techniques used by the teacher, the approach used, the impact this had on the students, and the key questions that will aid in the feedback conversations. Something like this helps maintain a clear focus during feedback conversations with the teacher and removes any judgment on the lesson. As you've guessed, I like using straightforward resources like this to do our job effectively, ones that can be adapted to achieve maximum impact.

What Isn't Helpful

Historically, teachers have been observed as part of their performance management cycle once or twice a year. This problem is because we know nothing is tying us down to putting any targets into practice. As long as we perform well on that day of the year, we pass our performance management observation and continue to teach in the way we have always done. One-off observation to tick a box does not give us the support we need to grow as practitioners. Furthermore, the feedback received varies depending on the observer. This makes observations less about helping teachers improve and more about checking up on what that teacher is doing.

As a teacher, I remember the anxiety that observations caused and how desperately I wanted my line manager to see how great a teacher I was. I also remember observation lessons going wrong. One observation in particular (where I was observed by two assistant heads – one being my line manager at the time and the other by the head of the faculty) stands out. Now, I'll be the first to confess that it wasn't the greatest lesson I have ever taught, but I still remember the feedback from my head of faculty, who made it their mission to tell me how poor my lesson was. This was not a typical lesson for me (but the observers did not know that), and I did not receive feedback that could move me forward in any helpful way. Observations and feedback like this are a hindrance and not a help.

I learnt nothing from the earlier observation (apart from how stressful the situation was), and I know I am not alone here. The problem with the lesson observation being carried out this way is that my attention was on the summative grade and my stand-alone performance of one lesson. It was not about where I was and where I needed to be as a teacher. The lesson feedback meeting gave me no opportunity to think for myself or ask the right questions about what would have helped me improve my teaching. What a mistake! I could accept this approach 10 and 15 years ago. But we now have more evidence telling us this doesn't work. High-stakes lesson observations of this nature cannot facilitate change in practice. Isn't it best to keep providing opportunities for us to develop as teachers and lesson observations that are low stakes? This can be a fantastic way to foster relationships and coaching conversations off the back of this.

Pause for Reflection

Think about the following list: Where are you currently? Where would you like to be? What might be stopping you from getting there? Building a learning culture for good lesson observations is one of the best ways to build trust among colleagues. Having an open-door policy where teachers are encouraged to pop into lessons and see how their peers teach is so powerful. As leaders, we need to make time for this to happen, and follow-up conversations between colleagues doing this are vital. The latter must happen. Otherwise, it eliminates the time given to talk about pedagogy. This is another reason why instructional coaching is so powerful: the time given after a lesson drop-in is factored in and cannot be missed.

Lesson Observations Should Be as Follows:	Lesson Observations Should Not Be as Follows:
• Learning opportunities are part of any CPD training offered to teachers. • Non-judgmental, with the teacher being encouraged to reflect on their teaching. Questions about 'How was that lesson for you?' are not helpful. • Post-lesson observation feedback should happen on the same day. • Bite-size feedback.	• One-off is where the observer tells the other person what to do. • Tick-box exercises that determine how good a teacher is in the classroom. • The feedback is not time-bound, with clear next steps and follow-up by the observer and observee. • Hierarchical and just completed by senior or middle leaders.

We know that when lesson observations are carried out as a learning opportunity and the observer is working for the observee, this becomes an opportunity for professional growth. If you haven't read 'Leverage Leadership' and are looking at ways to improve lesson observation feedback, I highly recommend you read Chapter 2. This has helped me identify how we can approach lesson observations and prompts me to think about providing effective feedback based on key elements of instructional coaching. I've provided an overview of this six-step feedback guide in Appendix 6, which should give you a good starting point. Many schools consider this a helpful framework, so I wanted to include it. However, as with anything you read, always frame feedback models based on what's suitable for your teachers, helping them become stronger practitioners for their pupils.

Addressing Barriers to Instructional Coaching

As school leaders, we face the difficult task of determining the most impactful interventions for our schools to enhance student achievement. Weighing up what to invest in that will have a significant impact, particularly what will help teachers become more effective, can be tricky, and we are not always going to get this right. I certainly haven't.

The type of coaching we offer, whether it is leadership coaching or instructional coaching, will only work if it aligns with a culture where there are high levels of trust. If this trust is not quite there and there is still a fear of getting things wrong, I would focus on removing this before investing in any type of coaching.

Equally, for instructional coaching to be effective and in line with our evidence, we need to recruit the right people to become coaches and then give them adequate resources to do the job effectively. Otherwise, just like those one-off INSETs where staff fail to engage because they have heard it all, the impact of something like instructional coaching will be short-lived. Additionally, in schools where lesson observations are primarily used for judgment rather than professional development, the introduction of teaching and learning coaching may be met with scepticism. The coaching approach empowers teachers to take ownership of their progress, which requires time and support. Carefully consider your school's culture. Are you ready for coaching? Or do you need to work on removing the fear culture first?

Experienced teaching and learning practitioners need to perform this role, and you need to release them from their everyday teaching commitments to provide sufficient time for them to work with teachers; otherwise, instructional coaching will not be effective. This is not appropriate if you expect instructional coaches to have meetings in their own time or during non-teaching contact time teaching.

Instead, show people you understand this is important and care about making this work. So if you haven't got the capacity to set this up in-house, a sensible option is to work with a trusted partner. Additionally, this can eliminate the fear of someone feeling judged by a colleague they work with daily. I realise there may be cost implications here with CPD budgets that have been massively squeezed in recent years, but if you feel it is the only way of fully committing to support a particular group of teachers properly, then it is worth investing in. Getting the right person to work with you is key, and I collaborate with schools that bring in external practitioners for such work, which proves to be extremely powerful if they are aligned with your vision and what you are trying to do. External coaching support also enables those working on the ground to concentrate on the everyday business of running a school.

Conclusion

For coaching to be effective, we need to deploy the right colleagues to do this and give them the right resources to coach effectively. Coaching should also sit side-by-side with any CPD programme. When a training programme is designed this way from the outset, the chances of success are very high. Colleagues will feel supported and encouraged along their professional journey – a win-win for all. We have also looked at the importance of instructional coaching and how this can be different to other forms of coaching in supporting teachers in developing their instruction. This can be particularly useful if we want to improve how we use classroom observations to support teachers in gaining maximal benefits or the time spent with a more experienced teacher. This is where I see the power of instructional coaching.

In the next chapter, we will focus on CPD evaluation and explore how we can measure the success of CPD activities in our schools. This will help us improve the quality of CPD initiatives and identify which types of CPD are positively impacting our schools.

Reflective Questions

1. To what extent are you implementing coaching as a form of continuing professional development for colleagues in your school?
2. Do you offer more coaching or mentoring in your school? How do you determine when and where to apply coaching versus mentoring?
3. Which 'golden principles' would you like to develop in your school?
4. How can coaching be part of all follow-up activities to any INSET or twilight training programme?

5. What resources and support do you provide coaches to carry out their role effectively?
6. How do teachers in your school collaborate with their colleagues to improve their teaching practice?
7. On a scale of 1-10 (10 being very effective and 1 being not effective at all), how are teacher classroom observations used to help teachers improve their teaching?
8. What resonates with you about instructional coaching as a concept?
9. How could you/are you developing instructional coaching in your school?
10. Which of the barriers to implementing instructional coaching are you most worried about?

Chapter Snapshots

- Coaching is valuable for professional development because it offers personalised support, encourages reflective practice, facilitates skill development, and nurtures a growth mindset.
- Historically, two distinct approaches have guided educational improvement: the pedagogical approach, which emphasises expertise through knowledge acquisition, and the developmental approach, rooted in coaching and continuous learning.
- Mentoring and coaching share similarities, both being valuable CPD tools for educators. It's essential to recognise when to employ each approach.
- The role of coaching in schools has evolved, shifting from primarily addressing underperformance to enhancing the knowledge and skills of school leaders and teachers.
- Coaching is most effective when integrated with other CPD activities and should not be offered in isolation.
- Coaches should receive proper training and sufficient time to perform their roles effectively.
- Successful coaching for CPD thrives in a culture of trust, collaboration, and a willingness to learn from mistakes.

- Understanding transactional analysis (TA), explicitly staying in the adult ego state, is crucial for effective coaching conversations.
- Instructional coaching focuses on enhancing teaching and learning. Unlike traditional coaching, it emphasises more than just asking questions and can be transformative for school lesson observations.
- Jim Knight's 'Impact Cycle' offers a practical framework for effectively implementing instructional coaching. It revolves around identifying an individual's needs, the learning process, and the specific strategies and actions for improvement. Additionally, Knight provides valuable ethical principles that should be adhered to for instructional coaching to succeed.

References

Bambrick-Santoyo, P. and Lemov, D. (2018) *Leverage leadership 2.0: A practical guide to building exceptional schools*. 2nd edition. San Francisco, CA: Jossey-Bass.

Beere, J., 2016. *Grow: Change Your Mindset, Change Your Life – A Practical Guide to Thinking on Purpose*. Crown House Publishing.

Berne, E. (1964) *Games people play: The psychology of human relationships*. New York: Grove Press.

Brighouse, T. (2006) *Essential pieces: The jigsaw of a successful school*. Milton Park: Research Machines.

Cheliotes, L.G. and Reilly, M.F. (2010) *Coaching conversations: Transforming your school one conversation at a time*. Thousand Oaks, CA: Corwin.

Downey, M. (2003) *Effective coaching: Lessons from the coaches' coach*. 2nd edition. New York: Texere Publishing.

Grant, V. (2014) *Staying a head: The stress management secrets of successful school-leaders*. London: Integrity Coaching.

Hargreaves, A. and Fullan, M. (2012) *Professional capital: Transforming teaching in every school*. New York: Teachers College Press.

Knight, J. (2018) *The impact cycle: What instructional coaches should do to foster powerful improvements in teaching*. Thousand Oaks, CA: Corwin.

Knight, J. (2021) *The definitive guide to instructional coaching: Seven factors for success.* Alexandria, VA: ASCD (ASCD member book).

Whitmore, J. (2017) *Coaching for performance: The principles and practice of coaching and leadership.* 5th edition. London, England: Nicholas Brealey Publishing.

7 The Evaluation of Continuous Professional Development

Most evaluations, when they take place at all, tend to use post-session 'happy sheets' that ask: 'Did you enjoy the CPD?' and 'How well was it presented?' While such questions are important, they belong in the first of five levels that Thomas Guskey considers an organisation must go through to measure the effectiveness of its CPD.

Leading CPD evaluation theorists like Guskey, Lieberman, and Knight have found that many schools, educators, and teachers don't evaluate the impact of CPD effectively. Sometimes, that's because they simply forget or they don't know how to.

Let's Pause!
How Do You Evaluate the Quality of CPD in Your School?

Perhaps you might do the following:

- Hand out a feedback sheet at the end of a training session (the most popular form of evaluation).
- Carry our classroom learning walks a week or two weeks after the chosen CPD.
- Arrange a meeting with a group of staff to discuss the CPD activity.

All important things, but is there more that can be done? Is the aforementioned enough to simply tell us if the professional development is working and having an impact? I'll leave this to you to decide.

Here are some ideas for why CPD evaluation doesn't always get done that I think we all relate to.

DOI: 10.4324/9781003232179-7

- Lack of time
- Lack of money
- Difficult to measure
- Lack of knowledge and expertise
- Unreliable data

Evaluating the Impact of CPD

The good news is that we are talking a lot more about the impact of professional development in our schools, which goes hand in hand with CPD evaluation. I would like to emphasise early on that when we are considering CPD evaluation, our attention should be directed towards finding 'evidence' rather than 'proving' its success. Obtaining evidence holds significant importance for three main reasons. Firstly, it provides us with essential information about which aspects of professional development are effective and what needs improvement, whether it's a stand-alone programme or CPD taking place over an extended period. Secondly, having evidence allows us to see firsthand which CPD training supports raise standards in our schools, thereby adding value, and which ones are not. Thirdly, focusing on obtaining evidence helps us lay the groundwork for evidence-based change and clarifies why such change is necessary.

This is something I'm always talking about in my initial meetings with schools and where we look at the aims of the training and how we are going to capture the impact this has across the school. This, for me, is so important because it justifies the purpose of any training and helps move us all to move in the right direction in alignment. My ideas around evaluating professional development largely come from the work of Thomas Guskey (2000). For anyone interested in developing their knowledge further after this chapter, I would encourage you to add 'Evaluating Professional Development' to your reading list. It provides a very useful insight into the type of data we can gather from a CPD activity that enables us to know what's working as well as what needs improving. And in this chapter, I will focus on how we can do just this. And yes, we are probably all at different stages

The Evaluation of Continuous Professional Development

with this, but what I feel is essential is that we build CPD evaluation when we are planning our school CPD and work backwards from this.

By doing this, we'll then know if the CPD has been meaningful and truly met its aims. But how can we do this?

In this chapter, we will look at precisely this and determine the following:

- What we mean by the term 'evaluation' and the difference between summative and formative evaluations.
- The different ways we can evaluate CPD and use these findings to improve both the quality of CPD provision on offer, its impact, and success.
- How to apply Thomas Guskey's five-step evaluation framework.
- Provide tools that will help you plan and implement effective CPD evaluations in your schools.

As you read on, I am hoping to give you an insight into how we can begin to evaluate CPD in our school that moves beyond participants' feedback forms at the end of a session/s. This may appear daunting or difficult, but it doesn't need to be. I also believe in baby steps. So you can start with one or two of the ideas I'll mention on evaluating your CPD activities and building on it over two or three years. Remember when we mentioned the small marginal gains? Well, use this approach if you are looking to improve how you evaluate CPD in your school. Think back to what we said about the key ingredients we need for building good habits, and simply apply the same formula when designing, planning, and evaluating CPD. If you are reading this as a CPD leader/school leader, you should find many helpful ways to carry out CPD evaluation in your school. If you are reading this as a teacher, hopefully, this will explain how CPD evaluation is more than just completing an end-of-session questionnaire. The truth is that when evaluating CPD, we largely base this on just one perspective. However, the ideas covered here will provide you with food for thought on how we can approach this differently. They work for me, so I am hoping you will feel the same and be able to use the resources and examples.

Great Professional Development That Leads to Great Pedagogy

I often get asked what makes an effective CPD model. I don't think there is a clear-cut answer, and the research we have on effectiveness tells us that CPD needs to be delivered over two or three terms, focused on student outcomes, clear learning outcomes from the start, and enable teachers to work together.

If we are going to design effective and purposeful CPD in our schools, then I would say we need to be asking our staff what they feel makes good CPD and base our model on this. When was the last time you asked your colleagues this question? Are they even consulted? We often read about what makes good CPD in our schools, and I've provided quite a few examples and ideas of my own so far, but what do the people in your school think about this themselves? Have you ever obtained such feedback when looking at improving the quality of professional development and including activities that matter to your staff? If we are going to design CPD that is meaningful and one that supports professional growth, then I think it's fair for all those leading CPD to assess where we are in this process. Do we consult staff in such discussions, or are we just providing them with mere evidence from other sources in the hope that they are convinced by what we are telling them? I'll let you think and decide where you are with this. If you are looking to improve your CPD staff provision in your school or design a CPD model that works for you, then I would urge you to gain quite a bit of information from all your staff on what they feel makes effective CPD. And by all your staff, I really do mean everyone: admin, HR, support teachers. You can see where I am going with this. Make the aim of the exercise clear, and share your findings and outcomes. Doing this will help you identify staff views towards not only professional learning but also what they find helpful that you should consider. Just like Veema's CPD model I mentioned in Chapter 2, it includes the four key components of **'consult, tailor, train, and reflect,'** which is clear to use, and each step has a key role to play in evaluating the effectiveness of the CPD programme. Create a CPD model that shows your whole-school community the value you place

The Evaluation of Continuous Professional Development 145

on CPD, staff development (i.e. investing in them no matter what position they hold in the school), and how you give feedback. From this, you can build good evaluations, which are shared with everyone.

If you are looking for a simple but highly effective activity that gives you some informative feedback on the type of professional development colleagues in your school find effective and least effective, you may find the CPD questionnaire on the next page a useful starting point when trying to gauge staff attitudes towards CPD. Completing a short questionnaire like this can be very helpful when you are trying to assess attitudes towards CPD and what your staff find useful or not. As I mentioned at the beginning of this chapter, CPD evaluation can often be ignored, mostly because we've not thought about it in the first place. This is why I feel it is helpful for this to be considered when designing your CPD provisions. Even if this isn't perfect the first time around, you can always look at ways of improving it. I also feel that a simple short activity like the one earlier at the start of a meeting is quite an easy thing to do with all staff and has the potential to give us so much valuable information. It also enables us to involve staff in this process, taking a bottom-up approach to the changes we are making – a vital buy-in and one that helps control the top-down gremlin.

Before we explore the evaluation of CPD in greater depth, I wanted to begin by outlining, first of all, how a simple evaluation exercise of this nature can be the first step we take to gain feedback on professional development, distinguishing what your staff feels makes effective and not-so-effective professional development.

CPD evaluation is something I became interested in around 2017. I have to be honest and say that before this, I didn't know much about what this involved, apart from handing out an evaluation form at the end of a training event, which can often serve for summative purposes. Now I'm not saying this isn't important; however, if this is the only way we are capturing feedback from a CPD programme, then we must strive to do more. Furthermore, I don't believe that all CPDs need to be evaluated in the same way. It should be up to the school to decide how and what they choose to evaluate as long as it gives them enough information to assess the impact this has on teachers. For example, a

146 A School Leader's Guide to Leading Professional Development

Table 7.1 Whole-Schol Professional Development Survey

Professional Development Exercise

Use the following short questionnaire to gain the views and experiences of staff and teachers in your school towards the most effective (best) and least effective (worst) professional development programme they have been involved with. This should help you when designing the type of CPD your colleagues feel is most effective in helping them improve their knowledge, skills, and practice.

Instructions

Describe the characteristics of the most effective (best) and least effective (worst) professional development programme you have been involved with.

Question	Most Effective	Least Effective
Programme topic		
Who planned the programme?		
Who participated?		
Who led the programme (senior or middle leader, external provider)?		
How large was the participant group?		
When was it held?		
How long was it?		
What types of activities were involved?		
Did it involve changes in the classroom or whole-school practice?		
How extensive were those changes?		
How difficult were the changes to implement?		
Were follow-up activities involved?		
Who led the follow-up activities?		
What improvements did the programme bring?		

safeguarding and child protection training course may be evaluated differently from a leadership training course we are running for our middle leaders. For example, we may feel that a short questionnaire followed by a series of short safeguarding quizzes every four to five weeks may be sufficient in providing you with meaningful information about the impact of your whole-staff safeguarding training, whereas the methods you use to assess learning could look very different. This is perfectly fine. Evaluating CPD does not need to be carried out in the same way for all CPD activities. It should not be complicated or taxing of people's time. Rather, it should be well planned, informative, and up to those involved to decide how they do this. I'm hoping that by the end of this chapter, you will get to see why I believe this.

Standard for Teachers' Professional Development

In July 2016, the DfE published the Standards for Teachers' Professional Development, which aimed to give all those responsible for teacher professional development further guidance on what makes effective CPD. The guidance sets out five key strands that should be used in conjunction with the teachers' standards that schools should follow. Each standard should provide a tool for self-reflection on current practices and stimulate discussions between teachers, headteachers, leadership teams, and other professionals who provide and support professional growth.

To fully utilise these CPD standards, it would be useful to develop a practical CPD audit tool that helps us capture where we are based on each recommended standard. A template for this has been included on the next page. This is another way to evaluate your school's CPD and should help you benchmark this across the DfE standards and their guidance.

This is just one example that may help you, and I'm not saying should only come from one source; however, like any audit, it does provide a useful tool for assessing where we might be regarding some of the research evidence. For each of the teachers' professional development standards, I have created a set of statements that you can use to assess where you might be with a simple RAG rating. Doing this will help you assess and evaluate your current position on CPD in your school as well as what you might like to be in the future.

Before we look at improving our current CPD provision, we'll need to assess where we are. There is no point in throwing everything away and starting from scratch! Unless all your staff has elected this, this sort of change doesn't need to happen. Instead, try to figure out what CPD your staff find effective and not and whether your staff's CPD provisions are in line with reliable sources like those I've mentioned from the EEF and the Centre for the Use of Research and Evidence in Education (CUREE).

And remember, when we are looking at improving anything in our schools, there is more than one way of doing this. Adapt anything and everything to suit your school content. When we don't do this, I believe it limits our thinking and creativity and can be dangerous to our goal. Remember, what works for one school does not necessarily work for another, and we must have evidence behind our rationale.

By doing this, we can create a picture of what CPD in our school looks like in relation to some of the evidence that is out there. Such activities are incredibly useful, as they give us a moment to reflect on our current position and what our next steps might look like. Additionally, when thinking about CPD evaluations, this does not only refer to evaluating a programme, activity, seminar, or event. CPD evaluations should also include obtaining important information and evidence on how we plan, design, and monitor CPD to ensure it has all the ingredients to be successful. Think back to the 14 mechanisms of effective professional development given to us by the EEF. Have you ever carried out an evaluation of this in your school to determine the extent to which these mechanisms are incorporated into your professional development? Doing this will enable us to keep improving our CPD provision, and this is why evaluating professional development is so important. In doing this, we continue to help teachers improve and get better. Before we take a look in more detail at different methods we can use to evaluate CPD, I would first like to explore what we mean by the term 'evaluation.'

What Is Evaluation?

The job of a school leader is never done, and a big part of knowing what works well in our schools and for our pupils comes down to the evaluation methods we carry out. As school leaders and teachers, we evaluate the work we do all the time, both formally and informally, and both serve their purpose when this is done for the right reasons! Good evaluations require careful planning, thought, and an understanding of how we find valid and reliable answers. Like many colleagues, I have a big issue when school evaluation practices aren't done for the correct reasons and by the right people. When done simply to prove someone's capability or merely for summative purposes used for commercial purposes, it does not help us in the long run. Before we look more closely at how to approach the evaluation of CPD, let us first decide what evaluation is.

Table 7.2 Professional Development Audit (RAG Exercise)

Assess your CPD design and implementation in your school by utilising this audit based on the DfE's professional development standards. Review each statement with your team or yourself to determine where you stand on the five sections provided.

CPD Standards	Profession Development Statement	Red	Amber	Green
1. Professional development should have a focus on improving and evaluating pupil outcomes	• Our objectives for student outcomes are clear when designing/implementing CPD. • Our objectives for student outcomes are shared with all participants. • The links between activities and intended outcomes are explicit. • Activities take into account teachers' starting points and intended progression. • Activities are always evaluated against their impact on student outcomes. • Formative assessment of activities is continually applied to monitor progression and impact. • Complimentary activities are chosen and linked clearly to objectives and intended impact. • Providers are clear on the intended impact on pupil outcomes. • Providers are given information on participants' knowledge, experience, and goals. • Tools to evaluate progression and impact are provided.			

(Continued)

Table 7.2 (continued)

CPD Standards	Profession Development Statement	Red	Amber	Green
2. Professional development should be underpinned by robust evidence and expertise	<ul><li>Expert input explores how and why practices work across different contexts.</li><li>Links to robust evidence are made clear.</li><li>Teachers are given the opportunity to practice and feedback with links to pupil outcomes.</li><li>Teachers actively seek formative evaluation of the impact of new practices.</li><li>Input constructively challenges participants' existing beliefs.</li><li>Teachers can adapt generic pedagogic practices for different subjects and contexts.</li><li>Independent evaluations demonstrate the impact of the programme on student outcomes.</li></ul>			
3. Professional development should include collaboration and expert challenge	<ul><li>Expert support and challenge are sought throughout the programme.</li><li>Experts provide multiple opportunities to support teachers' practice and evaluation.</li><li>Professional development activities include external challenge to thinking.</li><li>Activities allow the adaptation of approaches for the classroom through practice.</li><li>Structured collaboration and discussion about the impact on pupils is supported.</li><li>Participants are encouraged to analyse evidence from classroom implementation.</li><li>Practices with peers and focus discussions on the impact on pupils are implemented.</li><li>External perspective/s is used to challenge current orthodoxies, raise expectations, and introduce evidence-informed practices.</li></ul>			

4. **Professional development programmes should be sustained over time**	- Programmes typically last at least two terms and provide ongoing support.
- The commitment required by teachers and school leaders is clear, leading to sustained changes in practice.
- Activities of shorter duration (e.g. one day) are either focused on a narrow goal or form part of coherent sequences to achieve broader goals.
- Ideas are translated into relevant practice and knowledge for specific classes and pupils.
- Time is made for ongoing practice and review.
- Experts link shorter activities with sustained programmes and provide ongoing support.
- Other work pressures do not detract from the achievement of professional development objectives.
- Supporting components (e.g. venues, rooms, refreshments) do not detract from the achievement of professional development.
5. **Professional development must be prioritised by leadership**	- Evidence-informed development is a major leadership priority.
- Teachers take responsibility for their own professional development.
- External support is used to develop effective school leadership systems and processes.
- A culture of trust, professional engagement, and challenge is built using evidence and knowledge.

(Continued)

Table 7.2 (Continued)

CPD Standards	Profession Development Statement	Red	Amber	Green
	• We engage openly in a discussion/s about the impact of teaching practice with peers and leaders supporting a culture of trust, respect, and scholarship. • School leaders and participants are challenged to be clear about their requirements; tools and resources are offered to support this. • School, subject, phase, and individual development plans are coherent and supported. • We are fully committed to effective professional development practices; we challenge poor or ineffective ones. • We are explicit about the role of teachers and school leaders before and after the programme.			

Let's Think About This for a Moment!

If we were sitting in a room working through these ideas together and I asked you to define the word 'evaluation,' what would you write?

As you take a moment to reflect on this, I've included some words that are often associated with the term 'evaluation' in a cloud bubble below (Figure 7.1). Which of these words resonates with you the most? And why?

Figure 7.1 Key Terms Associated with Evaluation

In education, we carry out evaluations to determine the value and usefulness of an approach we take or an intervention we set up and to measure the impact of this. We tend to do this by collecting various information that informs, guides, and assesses how successful or good this has been.

Effective CPD evaluation models should gather sound, reliable, and meaningful information needed to make more thoughtful, responsible decisions. As I mentioned earlier, sound evaluations help us answer key questions by collecting relevant information and evidence on the work we are doing. It informs our practice, enables us to reach conclusions, and holds us accountable. Accountability is a good thing. Knowing what works in our school, classroom, or with a certain group of students is a very good thing and part of being a reflective practitioner. Being able to communicate this is equally important.

Lots of teaching pedagogies and approaches work in education. This isn't a new phenomenon. Well-regarded educators such as Dylan William, John Hattie, and Mary Myatt have highlighted this for some time now. From all the great teaching methodologies or school approaches that we know, what's important for us is to work out what works best for our kids and the whole-school community. Where we just keep doing more of this. Being able to work this out comes from well-planned and meaningful school evaluations. But when it comes to evaluating the quality of professional development in your school, how and what do you do? Is this an area that is ignored, or does this inform an integral part of your CPD planning? I experience that many schools do not always know what or how to evaluate CPD to any great extent. This is not their fault, as many CPD leaders are never taught how to do this efficiently. I was equally in the same position.

Here Are Some Facts to Consider

> The logical chain found that few school leaders evaluated the impact of CPD on teaching and learning (Ofsted, 2006).
> Organisational change, value for money, and changes in teacher behaviour were less likely to be evaluated (Goodall et al., 2005).
> Research findings suggest that schools need more support and training in evaluating the impact of CPD.
> Most evaluations seem to draw on the teacher, which can be superficial and lead to biased results (Harris et al, 2006).

What does the previous section tell us about some of the evidence we have on CPD evaluations? You might read these statements and feel you are in a similar position at your school or that you are working hard to improve how you do this.

What's important here is that we understand the following:

- Why do we evaluate professional development?
- How do we evaluate professional development?
- What factors do we take into account when we evaluate professional development?

By thinking about these questions, we can start thinking about why measuring the impact of teacher CPD is important and what evidence we will collect to determine its effectiveness. This should include evaluating not just the content of a course/programme/event or enjoyability levels but also the long-term gains, such as the use of this new learning by teachers or the degree of organisational support and the impact this has on student achievement. A robust evaluation method that considers all these factors is essential. CPD evaluation serves two purposes.

Summative Evaluations

Summative evaluation happens at the end of the CPD programme and tends to give us a judgment and score to assess the success of the CPD.

Formative Evaluations

Formative evaluations look at obtaining ongoing information and data that improves the quality of the CPD.

Both types of evaluations are important. However, most evaluations of CPD tend to be summative to a large extent.

Why do you think this is? Take a moment to think about this, and you may even like to jot this down somewhere on a Post-it note and come back to this conversation starter with your colleagues.

Anyhow, you might be thinking the reason for this includes some, if not all, of the following:

- I don't know where to start apart from designing a feedback survey.
- It's not important to our school.
- We barely have time to cover the CPD areas we've selected as a school to now focus on an additional layer that involves ongoing evaluation.

I accept all viewpoints on this matter. For CPD evaluations to be effectively carried out, they need to be incorporated as part of the CPD planning and not just added at the end as a stand-alone activity. This needs some thinking, and one of the reasons why we do not always apply sophisticated methods for evaluating professional development stems from the ideas I have included earlier.

But there's no point in just mentioning the problems if we are not going to provide helpful suggestions on overcoming some of these barriers. Therefore, I will suggest we consider the following five key principles when evaluating CPD. There could be more, but these are my five key ideas, and you are welcome to create your own and share your ideas with me on social media.

Key Idea 1: Design CPD With Evaluation in Mind

This is one of the most important and easiest things you can do to ensure that evaluation is not missed. Always start with the end in mind where you have clear PD learning objectives for each CPD session alongside these one or two evaluation methodologies.

Let's say, for example, that you are running the English department in your school and are receiving training on how to effectively support year 7 students in reading and writing due to the loss of learning that has taken place from COVID. When planning the training, you identify from the onset what and how you will evaluate the success of your training. I've provided an example of this later, which can be adapted and used for any CPD activity. Planning in this way will not only show you what's working well but also make your CPD count. The first three columns have been left blank to help you personalise this according to your focus.

Key Idea 2: Focus on Teachers and Students

Focus on measuring the difference CPD makes to teacher practice and student outcomes rather than the activity itself. Teachers who teach effectively aspire to deepen their craft. CPD evaluations enable teachers to improve their skills, knowledge, and classroom practice. Students should benefit because of this, and evaluating CPD in this way should give us the information we require to assess whether we are doing exactly this.

Key Idea 3: Avoid Subjectivity!

When thinking about CPD evaluations, try to move away from just taking information from one point of view. This can skew the validity and reliability of your data and cannot always reflect what is really going on. For example, a teacher could tell us how they are using a

Table 7.3 Reading and Writing Training Programme

Five-Week PD Programme for English Teachers

PD Title	Learning Outcomes	Resources	Organisational Support	Evaluating Impact
S1			Team teaching time allocated to co-planning lessons. SOW and lesson plans are shared amongst the team.	• Staff evaluation form to be handed out at the end of S1. • Teachers agree to team teaching, and coworking groups are formed with agreed meeting times.
S2				• Teacher interviews/questionnaires were sent out up to seven days after the training to assess participants' learning of new knowledge and understanding.
S3				• Teacher peer group discussion at the end of the training to see what parts of the training programme support their teaching this group of students and what needs to be adapted for S4 and 5.
S4				• Classroom observations on using the teaching techniques from the training.
S5				• Review of students' work. • Feedback from students through the use of questionnaires/samples of students' work.

particular teaching strategy and how well it is going, but when you discuss this with their students or during lesson observations, you fail to see it. Evaluations should come from various sources. When we do this, it will help us truly understand the impact the professional development has had as well as improve anything that may not have worked so well.

Key Idea 4: Quantitative and Qualitative Methods

Evaluating CPD should always be about knowing what's working or worked and what we need to improve. I'll be looking more at this on page 165, but the methods of data you will collect should include both quantitative and qualitative methods taken from questionnaires, interviews, low-stake lesson observations among peers, and student data. When we do this, the information we get provides a holistic picture of where we are rather than just reviewing the CPD activity itself, which defeats the purpose of why we evaluate the first place. Additionally, what can also be a complete waste of time is when CPD quantitative evaluations only serve the organisation's purpose. As brilliant as we all might be (which we are, I don't doubt this), this doesn't help and just adds to the workload of the person responsible for designing the feedback form and the time of the people completing the form.

Idea 5: Share Your Findings

How often do you share the findings you have received from the CPD that is delivered at your school? In my experience, the outcomes we share tend to be done at review meetings that mainly benefit senior leaders and external stakeholders. If this is something you do, then I suggest you think about how you can do this differently. For me, this is a vital principle for knowing what is working well and what needs to be improved. This should be showcased at staff meetings, teaching and learning bulletins, and when staff come together for the CPD activity.

These five principles provide you with some guidance on the different areas you need to take into account when assessing the value and purpose of CPD in your school. I've provided some simple but vital

The Evaluation of Continuous Professional Development 159

dos and don'ts in the following table that support the principles I've covered in this section. Again, this is not an exhaustive list, but they should navigate your thinking process and help you have some good discussions with colleagues.

Bearing the previous section in mind, the next section will focus on how we can use Guskey's five levels of professional development evaluation. When looking at this, you need to do what works for your school. Some of this might be very new, and you'll probably need some additional support. You should not approach this alone, even if you are the CPD leader. I certainly approached this with much consideration, and there's nothing wrong with taking small baby steps at the

Table 7.4 Summary Table: Evaluating the Impact of CPD on Your School: Dos and Don'ts.

Dos	Don'ts
Use Guskey's five-level framework to evaluate your professional development. Try starting with level 5 first and working backwards.	Don't see evaluation as an 'add-on' to the back end of a CPD programme. It should be embedded throughout the process.
Plan how you will evaluate CPD's impact right from the start.	Don't see CPD evaluations as just a job for the senior leadership team. It's a job for everyone.
Know what you want children to learn differently because of the CPD.	Don't just evaluate participants' perceptions, as this could lead to bias and very subjective results.
Use a range of quantitative and qualitative data for evaluation, such as questionnaires, interviews, focus group meetings, observations, feedback sheets, and reflection logs.	Don't make CPD evaluations burdensome. With the right training, a practical and collaborative approach, and the use of the right tools, this can become a quite straightforward process.
Carefully consider the nature of the questions you use to assess the impact of CPD so the answers provide real insight.	Don't start any evaluation until you have an understanding of how the information will be gathered and used.
Focus on measuring the difference CPD makes to teacher practice and student outcomes, rather than the activity itself.	
Involve all participants in the evaluation process from the beginning.	

start to work out what you can do. Have in mind the purpose of the evaluation activity/ies and what you would like to achieve.

Applying Guskey's Five Critical Levels of Professional Development Evaluation

I believe that the appeal of Guskey's ideas lies in allowing us to garner both summative and formative feedback, which helps facilitate our professional development as teachers/or school leaders. Acknowledging the significance of proper CPD in raising academic standards, particularly its effects on teaching and learning that result in enhanced student outcomes, it becomes even more essential for us to incorporate such criteria into our assessment system. In appendices 1, 2, and 3, I've included example questionnaires and interviews you can use if you use Guskey's five levels of CPD evaluation. By referring to Guskey's five levels, I feel we can carry out the following:

- a detailed and more sophisticated evaluation exercise of professional development that is not only focused on participants' reactions to the CPD
- a more in-depth evaluation over a longer period of time; in Appendix 1, I have laid out a schedule that will give enough time for comprehensive evaluations; this timeline may be modified depending on the particular CPD requirements
- vital changes to the CPD before it has finished
- meaningful observations/interviews, etc., to determine whether the CPD has informed classroom practice and student outcomes
- an analysis of whether money has been well spent

Level 1 - Evaluate Participants' Reactions

Mechanism

End-of-session questionnaires/interviews.

Purpose

To gauge levels of baseline satisfaction to improve programme design and delivery. This is the most popular form of evaluation and refers back to the happy surveys I mentioned at the beginning of the chapter. Evaluating participants' reactions is very important and gives us some vital information on the success of professional development. At this level, questions must focus on the contents (course material), process (how the course was delivered), and context (the environment). Getting such feedback is invaluable to the success of professional development and will determine what participants do next and is vital for implementation. This should be taken straight after the professional development event.

Key Questions

1. Enjoyable?
2. Valuable?
3. Understandable?
4. Was the presenter knowledgeable?
5. Relevant learning aims/course material?
6. Useful?
7. Time well spent?
8. Good refreshments?
9. Correct room temperature?
10. Chairs comfortable?

How Will the Information Be Used?

- To improve programme delivery and design.

Level 2 - Evaluate Participants' Learning

Mechanism

Pen-and-paper exercises, questionnaires, interviews, simulations, demonstrations, participant reflection logs, or portfolios of work.

Purpose

To measure the knowledge and skills that participants acquired during professional development to assess what's actually been learnt. We must assess what new learning occurred so that every participant has a true learning experience. At this level, we attempt to identify what participants have learnt and retained. They may have enjoyed the professional training and engaged in meaningful conversations, but did they really learn anything? Evaluating their understanding is essential for validating what was intended to be achieved.

Questions at this level should relate to these learning objectives:

Cognitive: Have participants comprehended the rationale behind a teaching methodology and any fresh ideas?

Psychomotor: Do they have the capability to do something with their newfound knowledge? How much do they understand? Are they able to make adjustments?

Affective: Did the CPD alter their attitudes in some way? What kind of different behaviours would you like them to exhibit now?

Key Questions

- Did participants gain the knowledge and skills that were intended?
- What were the most important ideas you gained from this professional development?
- What key concepts did you take away from the professional development?
- Have you gained any tools that will help you better instruct students? Could you describe these abilities?

How Will the Information Be Used?

To improve programme content, format, and organisation.

Level 3 – Evaluate Organisation Support and Change

Mechanism

School records, minutes from meetings, questionnaires, and structured interviews with participants.

Purpose

To assess the organisation's levels of advocacy, support, accommodation, facilitation, and recognition so future change is more effective through better documentation and improved support. What support was provided by the organisation to initiate change and the support needed for participants to make full of their new knowledge and learning? What impact has the professional development had on the organisation?

Key Questions

- Effect on the organisation?
- Impact on organisational climate and procedures?
- Was implementation facilitated and supported?
- Allocated time and resources to support implementation?
- Problems solved quickly and efficiently?
- Sufficient resources made available?
- Successes recognised and shared?

How Will the Information Be Used?

- To document and improve organisational support.
- To improve future change efforts.

Level 4 - Evaluate Participants' Use of New Knowledge and Skills

Mechanism

Questionnaires, structured interviews with participants, participant reflection and portfolios, video and audio, as well as direct observation.

Purpose

To determine the depth and quality of implementation, it's important to observe what the participants have actually done as a result of the CPD. How have things changed, and how did the professional development impact their practice? This type of evidence cannot be gathered right away, as participants will need time for their new learning to take effect, create new habits, and get rid of old ones. Normally, several months would pass before any kind of understanding could be reached. To ensure that the information is not biased, the evidence must be collected from multiple sources in order to accurately gauge what has been achieved on levels 1-3.

Key Questions

- Did participants apply the new knowledge and skills effectively?
- What can be observed to show effective implementation is taking place?
- As a result of the CPD, what are you doing differently now than before?

How Will the Information Be Used?

To document and improve the implementation of programme content and to assess the value of time and money spent.

Level 5 - Evaluate Student Learning Outcomes

Mechanism

Student and school records, teacher classroom observations, participant portfolios, questionnaires, and/or structured interviews with students, parents, and teachers.

Purpose

Did the professional development programme actually impact students? Did it lead to any changes in student learning outcomes such as academic performance, attitude, mindset, as well as skills and behaviours? For this reason, we need to plan CPD with a focus on what students can get out of it rather than just its impact on teachers or the programme. Determining whether that goal has been achieved is naturally at the forefront of our minds. This emphasis on student outcomes is new but necessary because learners are the most important people involved.

Key Questions

- What is the impact on student performance and achievements like summative assessments and end-of-term grades?

- What is its influence on students' physical or emotional well-being?
- Are students more confident learners?
- Did student attendance improve? Or has the number of dropouts decreased?

How Will the Information Be Used?

Assess the impact the CPD has on student learning, improve the quality of the CPD, and assess the value of time and money spent.

Planning Effective CPD Evaluations

Considering Guskey's five levels, which you may or may not have been familiar with, think about which levels you are missing. How can these levels aid in evaluating your professional development? Ask yourself if the data you already use is enough to answer each of the questions associated with the level. If not, what adjustments do you need to make? In my work with schools on this issue, I have found it beneficial to focus on a school's CPD programme and analyse how its evaluation could better serve improvement. For example, research shows that most progress takes place at level 1 (participant reactions), right after or soon after a CPD programme has been carried out. However, this type of evaluation is brief and subjective, making it hard to figure out its true impact on the school, its teachers, and its students. It's important to look at our data about CPD evaluations and determine how we can put each level into practice, act upon them, and keep evidence to make our CPD worthwhile. In Appendix 4, there is an example timeframe that you can use to conduct CPD evaluations. This will help you determine appropriate timelines for when to undertake specific activities and the type of evaluation you can carry out. It is essential to decide on this from the outset, before any CPD activity takes place, and to make this known it to participants.

Paradigm Shift

Evaluation may seem daunting, causing it to be neglected in the CPD planning process, but it needn't be. One person, such as the CPD leader, should not conduct evaluations. This isn't beneficial. We should look to engage more people with the support of everyone in the school, particularly senior and middle leaders. At the start of the planning stage, everyone should know their involvement and the evidence that will be collected. This isn't about proving how 'great' or 'not good' we are but rather, facilitating meaningful conversations about the impact.

Additionally, fear should not hinder the process of obtaining evidence that may uncover undesirable results. Assessments that focus on how teachers implement and integrate new knowledge and learning from a professional development programme are invaluable for determining impact as well as the time and money spent. Investing in the process is about wanting to genuinely improve student learning and the quality of teaching at your school. The long-term commitment and critical planning needed for assessing the impact of CPD is crucial if we are to gain maximum benefit from training; measuring the effect of training is an integral step towards ensuring the best preparation and best outcomes. I'm hoping the areas we have covered in this chapter, along with the tools provided, will help when planning to evaluate the impact of your CPD during the evaluation process.

Conclusion

By carrying out strategically planned CPD evaluations, we can determine what's working well and what needs improvement. This assessment diet is essential if we want to measure the effectiveness of professional development and its impact on helping teachers become better educators and students learn more effectively. I decided to put it as the last chapter before my conclusion not because many of these ideas don't get done properly but rather because this is a key step in planning successful CPD training, and it can be hard. Hopefully, you'll recognise this isn't too difficult and understand the value a good CPD evaluation can offer your school's programme. If this part is missing from your plan, I hope I've provided you with the tools needed to start implementing evaluation on this degree. Let me know if you need any help getting started. In the final chapter, my summary will bring together all seven chapters and highlight the most important themes and ideas addressed at each stage, giving you, I hope, a CPD guidebook for 'leading a successful professional development.'

Reflective Questions

1. How do you currently evaluate CPD in your school?
2. What would you like to do differently when evaluating your CPD?
3. What further support and training do you need that will help you develop good CPD evaluations?
4. What is your understanding of summative and formative evaluations? Currently, which do you use more?
5. Why do CPD evaluations rarely get done?
6. How many of Guskey's levels of CPD do you use to evaluate the quality of CPD in your school? Is it realistic or even necessary to use all these levels?
7. How can we ensure that CPD evaluations are not solely subjective?
8. Do our evaluations vary depending on the kind of CPD activity taking place?
9. Does feedback from the evaluation have an effect on future CPDs?
10. Does the response from the CPD assessment shape overall school progress and planning?

Chapter Snapshots

- CPD evaluation typically includes a post-session feedback survey at the end of the session.
- Considering CPD evaluation justifies the purpose of any training and helps us all move in the right direction in alignment.
- Effective CPD evaluation models should gather sound, reliable, and meaningful information to make more thoughtful, responsible decisions. But do not begin any evaluation until you understand how the information will be collected and used.
- When evaluating CPD, start small and make incremental improvements over time, each term. If you are currently evaluating your CPD provision solely by completing end-of-session feedback sheets, consider conducting three or four teacher interviews two or three weeks after CPD events or utilising low-stakes lesson observations.
- We cannot just ignore CPD evaluation in schools due to fear of not knowing what to focus on or time constraints.

- CPD evaluation is vital to understanding which aspects of CPD work well, making valuable changes along the way to your CPD model, and assessing its impact on teacher practice and student achievement.
- Summative evaluation occurs at the end of the CPD programme and typically provides a judgment and score to assess the success of the CPD. On the other hand, formative evaluations focus on obtaining ongoing information and data to improve the quality of CPD. Both types of evaluations are important.
- In July 2016, the DfE published the Standards for Teachers' Professional Development (Department for Education, 2016) to provide further guidance to those responsible for teacher professional development on what constitutes effective CPD.
- Thomas Guskey's five levels of professional development offer a solid framework for the evaluation of CPD, where he explores participants' reactions to CPD (level 1), participants' learning (level 2), organisational support (level 3), participants' use of new learning (level 4), and student outcomes (level 5).
- Organisational change, value for money, and changes in teacher behaviour were less likely to be evaluated (Goodall et al., 2005).
- When evaluating CPD in your school, in addition to using Guskey's framework, keep in mind these five key principles: 1. design your CPD with evaluation in mind, 2. focus on teachers and students, 3. avoid subjectivity in evidence, 4. use both quantitative and qualitative methods to collect evidence, and 5. share outcomes with the school.

References

Department for Education (2016) *Standard for teachers' professional development, GOV.UK*. Available at: https://www.gov.uk/government/publications/standard-for-teachers-professional-development.

Goodall, J. et al. (2005) *Evaluating the impact of continuing professional development: Research*. London: Department for Education and Skills, p. 206.

Guskey, T.R. (2000) *Evaluating professional development*. Thousand Oaks, CA: Corwin.

Guskey, T. R. (2002). Professional development and teacher change. *Teachers and Teaching: Theory and Practice*, 8(3/4), 381-391.

Harris, J. et al. (2006) *Irish in primary schools: Long-term national trends in achievement*. Dublin: Stationery Office (Catalogue lists (Ireland. Stationery Office)).

Ofsted (2006) *The logical chain: Continuing professional development in effective schools*. London: Ofsted.

8 Conclusion

It's 5:06 pm on Wednesday, January 3, 2024. Remember how I started? It was Thursday, January 27, 2022, at 4 pm. Sometimes, it feels like I haven't moved from my computer. Writing the book has taken me on and off for just under two years. Not quite the deadline I set for myself or with the publishing company (sorry about that), but I've made it, and more importantly, I hope you, as readers, have too. Getting all my ideas down on paper has been an interesting journey – messy writer's heads, revising chapters, updating and deleting, piecing everything together. What a task, and what I've enjoyed most is having the time to put all my ideas and beliefs about what I think makes effective CPD all in one place.

My friend and colleague Lisa Jane Ashes advised me about the writing process. 'Just get writing, and the rest will come' was my inner voice when the words were not coming out on paper. I have to confess I wasn't as optimistic about writing to begin with, but Lisa was right (though we don't need to tell her this)! Lisa has extensive experience in this domain, and if you haven't read her book 'Teacher in the Cupboard,' it is another worthwhile read.

Once I got started (although I did need to pause the writing for a while), I wanted to get back to it because my confidence grew. I am sure many of you feel the same. The final submission deadline was always at the back of my mind; however, this became less important to me because I felt that my ideas and the research evidence I am aware of could be helpful to those school leaders and teachers who are looking to sharpen their CPD lens and dare to do things differently.

Some of my ideas may already be familiar to you. In a recruitment and retention crisis, we know just how important it is to do things differently to recruit and retain the right teachers for our kids. No school leader wants their school to invest in things just to tick a box or because they are educational fads. We might think we do, but behind being compliant, we know that most of what we do is for the good of our school community. When it isn't, simply stand your ground as much as possible and justify why you are not going to do it. At the end of the day, we are the experts, and we know what's best for our young people. Of course, our decision-making process should be informed by those around us and, above all, our moral compass.

In the UK, I am proud to have great professional development available to school leaders and teachers and amazing educational research to inform our practice. Many countries model our approach. This is great, and we need to celebrate this. We must ensure that we offer teachers professional development that we know works and allows them to grow and improve. After all, can we call it development if the person has done nothing with their new learning, knowledge, and skills? For teachers to do this, it is up to us as school leaders to create the conditions necessary.

One of the key messages in this book that you should take away is that good teacher professional development means higher student achievement rates. Leaving teachers to figure things out for themselves, engaging in random professional development here and there or with no continuation, and working in isolation won't make a difference.

Pause for Reflection

What are your key takeaways from the book?
What chapter resonates with you the most and will help you implement changes to your current CPD provision in your school?

Professional development has played a vital role in my career. I climbed the career ladder quickly with a strong desire to be a good teacher. Although some aspects of my personal life took a hit at the time, I was surrounded by like-minded professionals who encouraged and supported me.

Even in my current role at Veema, I believe in having a coach and mentor (I don't have all the answers, and I know this). Engaging with my own professional development allows me to get better at what I do. For me to support others, I need to have high expectations for myself to keep learning new things. This approach keeps me fresh, relevant, and in my challenge sweet spot. Clearly, I advocate for others to do the same.

When you leave a full-time teaching post, scepticism often arises from colleagues about one's ability to stay up-to-date and relevant. I've been faced with comments like 'That's all well and good, but you are not teaching full-time anymore,' and I have to say there is some truth in this. While I no longer work full-time in a school, it's crucial that when working with school leaders and teachers, I can demonstrate that I am the right person to support them, and I haven't forgotten what it is like to be in the school day. Schools are busy places, and there is so much that happens that you just can't plan for. Parents are demanding to speak with you, Jonny has left the building, or the fire alarm goes off during lunchtime. This is why I am also a strong advocate for the very best training coming from those who have been teachers. So when I work with schools, it is important that CPD training occurs in various formats, from traditional training to practical elements such as in-class teaching, working with students, coaching, and mentoring. Anyone can give advice and read statistics off a screen, but demonstrating it, in reality, is another matter and showing you can walk the talk. I strive to do the latter as much as possible.

Pause for Reflection

How do you share your professional development journey with colleagues at your school?

The Case for High-Quality CPD

In each chapter, I have presented the key elements essential for delivering high-quality CPD to teachers in our schools. We began by emphasising why this is so important, delving into the research evidence for why teacher quality matters, and explaining why this can't be compromised. When it occurs, students will simply suffer, and our teachers may soon leave us.

Therefore, establishing a robust culture of professional learning and involving teachers in high-quality CPD stands out as one of the most evidence-based and cost-effective strategies for increasing academic achievement. A key aspect of this offering is enhancing teachers' subject knowledge, pedagogical skills, and classroom practices, aiming to cultivate positive habits that contribute to better student learning and foster more confident teachers.

The Key Message

CPD should be informative, engaging, and challenging, enabling our teachers to acquire new information, enhance their existing subject and pedagogical knowledge, and demonstrate its practical application in the classroom. The same principle applies to leadership training. When learning new ideas about effective leadership, it's crucial to assess relevance in one's context and explore practical applications. It's always easy to say that something doesn't apply; in most cases, we have to problem-solve to see if we can find ways to use it.

In providing practical tips and suggestions, such as a good behaviour management strategy to use or advice for having successful difficult conversations with a colleague, I tend to follow these steps:

- Explain the strategy and how to use it.
- Present the reasons why it works, supported by the evidence available to us.
- Model the strategy in a variety of settings.
- Encourage individuals to consider how they can use or modify it.

This approach encourages others to consider the information presented and contribute their own perspectives thoughtfully.

When I deliver CPD training, I make the point somewhere in a session to mention that CPD should not be treated as a purely enjoyable event or get-together (I'm not a party pooper, I promise you). While everyone needs to have a good time and be engaged in the material, CPD is not about having a jolly, fun time. I prefer questions such as the following: What have you learned that you didn't know before? What will you do differently? What challenges are you facing at the moment regarding what's been discussed? How can you make this work for you?

This makes purposeful CPD and one that helps us plan training down to the T.

Successfully Designing and Planning Good CPD

The way we design CPD is crucial for its successful implementation and usefulness to teachers. This has been a key component of the book, and you should now have plenty of practical ideas along with reliable research on how people learn and develop professionally. I've also tried as much as possible to provide the key insights into how professional development activities need to be designed in schools to be meaningful, where people can actually see the benefits.

This is very important, remember the current data in this area, for example, where only a third of teachers in England typically take part in PD at least once a week and only 38% of teachers surveyed in October 2018 (EEF Professional Development Report) agreed that the 'time and resources available to them are used in a way that helps them improve their classroom practice'. When we read statistics like this, isn't it a wonder why most CPD initiatives fail to meet the desired goals?

So if we are going to change the statistics in this area, we really need to think hard about how we design and deliver professional development for teachers. The power to change is in our hands, and by incorporating the ideas covered in this book, I trust you've found plenty of material for contemplation.

Creating the right learning environment will enable us to support people in their development appropriately and demonstrate our value and investment in them. By considering some of the key messages and incorporating psychological theories such as Maslow's hierarchy of needs, the work of Matthew Kraft and John Papay, and more recent research from the EEF, we can reflect on what needs further development in our schools. And this cannot be left to one person, the CPD leaders. It requires school leaders to come together to develop a CPD model that is right for the school. It sounds challenging, but it doesn't need to be. So how much or how little from the following list are common features in your CPD provision?

- CPD INSET days and twilights are well-sequenced, with a common thread across all sessions.
- There are clear links between what has been covered before and what we are currently addressing. This involves revisiting previous material and managing the amount of information covered over time to avoid cognitive overload.
- The type of follow-up is made clear, and everyone knows what is expected of them before, during, and after a CPD session.
- Alongside the whole-school CPD priorities that everyone must follow, there is a choice of CPD sessions for teachers to choose from.
- Collaboration from a range of colleagues takes place regularly across the school, and meetings are effectively used to discuss teaching and learning.
- Any online CPD is followed up to check knowledge and understanding and identify learning gaps.
- There is a good balance of in-house and external CPD providers with a clear link between what everyone is working towards.
- Measure the impact of our CPD pre-, during, and post-CPD activities. This helps us improve provisions but also the quality of the activity itself.

Challenging Apathy

Like anything, we need to foster a culture in our schools that challenges disengagement and, to a large degree, conflict. On numerous occasions, I've witnessed school leaders aspiring to make changes. For these changes to succeed, they must invest in effective CPD. However, these efforts are often hindered by a lack of enthusiasm, both from those around them who may not recognise the need for change and external pressures stemming from constraints in time, money, and resources. We've all been there, and it's not easy, but we need to think creatively about overcoming these obstacles. We cannot, for example, avoid change simply because we fear it will be difficult or there isn't enough time for CPD.

Colleagues may become disengaged with CPD for the following reasons:

1. Their opinion has not been taken into account.
2. CPD is benchmarked against performance, creating a fear of pursuing it solely to meet summative goals.
3. They are given no time to think about professional development, and the limited time available is often when they may be overwhelmed at the start and end of the school year.
4. CPD is not relevant to their job role.
5. There is no accountability and follow-up.

If you are facing this issue, then perhaps you can think of the following:

Their Opinion Has Not Been Taken Into Account

Try This

- Sending out termly CPD questionnaires to help decide what CPD staff would prefer.
- Line managers/mentors regularly ask about the types of professional activities people would like to be involved in, individually or as part of school-wide initiatives. This approach provides ownership and individual responsibility, with individuals driving the process and facilitators supporting their choices.
- All staff are expected to lead a CPD activity throughout the school, either independently or in collaboration with a colleague.

CPD Is Often Benchmarked Against Performance, Creating a Fear of Pursuing It Solely to Meet Summative Goals

- Consider replacing performance management with a friendlier system, such as a professional growth model. This policy aligns more closely with the goal of cultivating excellent teachers, emphasising continuous improvement, and building and enhancing knowledge to bring about lasting changes in practice. Such poli-

cies take into account available research on creating better environments that enable sustained improvement.
- Establish a system that allows teachers to reflect on their successes, strengths, and areas for further growth against the teachers' standards or a similar framework used within your school. This system should enable teachers to seek feedback from more experienced staff and to make mistakes along the way without being perceived as a weakness.
- Eliminate any judgments associated with professional development. Utilise professional development as a means of continual improvement, focusing on the long-term benefits rather than short-term wins. Individuals should be encouraged to invest in this process not just because of what will be reflected in performance-related documents or CPD credits they receive but because it genuinely matters.

They are given no time to think about professional development, and the limited time available is often when they may be overwhelmed at the start and end of the school year.

Try this:

- Have a clear CPD programme schedule that precisely outlines what everyone will follow: who is doing what and when. This input should come from the teachers.
- INSET days should not only be about introducing new things. In fact, when the whole-school comes together, it is important that we celebrate and showcase the impact a CPD programme or activity is having.
- The most powerful thing we can do is to have teachers talk about pedagogy and their classroom practice. Your CPD provision to staff should include a substantial amount of this. Look for opportunities to incorporate it into your schedule.

CPD Is Not Relevant to Their Job Role Needs

Try This

- Ensure that everyone participating in the CPD activity actually needs to be there. If it's not relevant to their job role, question the necessity of their participation.

- When planning and delivering whole-school CPD, ensure that everything covered is relevant to all subjects within your curriculum. Provide numerous examples, and ask each department to showcase their ideas.
- Avoid offering the same old CPD that staff have heard before. Ensure that it is pitched at the right level and strikes the right balance.

There is no accountability and follow-up.

- Clearly articulate the journey, ensuring everyone understands what is expected of them and the direction of the training.
- Initiate follow-up actions from the start (with the flexibility to amend along the way), emphasising that CPD is not a stand-alone event.
- Understand that CPD is an opportunity for continuous improvement, not a quick fix for our challenges. This ethos should be ingrained in our culture and is an integral part of our roles as teachers, which is aimed at improving our professional practice for the benefit of our students. Regardless of our role in school, we are all committed to improving something, year in and year out.

When we strive to overcome some of the barriers mentioned earlier, which often hinder CPD from gaining the desired traction in our schools, I believe we can truly witness remarkable results. I have certainly observed this in my experience, and it is unquestionably an aspect that requires careful consideration when planning and designing professional development. If you aren't, what are you doing about it?

So as a final step (this is the last bit of big thinking I leave you with, I promise!), when you are evaluating where your current CPD provision is working for colleagues in your school and has a focus on improving student outcomes, which sections from the book do you need to focus your attention on? From this checklist, where would you place yourself for each statement and why? If you know you really should be a yes, then what is stopping you from doing this?

Short activities like the one earlier enable us to assess what needs to change or where we need to focus more attention. Remember, I

Table 8.1 CPD Audit Checklist

CPD Statements	Yes ✓	No ✓	Somewhat ✓	Examples of Where This Can Be Seen	RAG Rate
We utilise research to shape the design and planning of CPD activities and programmes.					
CPD is consistently maintained over time, providing frequent opportunities for learning, experimentation, practice, self-reflection, and evaluation. Honest and frequent feedback and solutions-focused conversations are integral components of our approach.					
Our approach focuses on evidence-informed practices, challenges existing assumptions, and centres around what works.					
Subject-based CPD meetings are scheduled at least once a month.					
Both novice and expert teachers have opportunities to collaborate and support each other.					
The entire school comes together for CPD sessions at least once every six weeks.					
Lesson observations contribute to CPD activities and serve as a means of assessing the effectiveness of practical strategies. Time is allocated afterwards for productive developmental conversations, aiming to support the observed teacher in becoming even better.					
Weekly directed time is allocated for professional development activities.					

(Continued)

Table 8.1 CPD Audit Checklist (Continued)

CPD Statements	Yes ✓	No ✓	Somewhat ✓	Examples of Where This Can Be Seen	RAG Rate
Formal qualifications are integrated into our CPD offerings for staff.					
Clear teaching standards are in place, providing a framework for teachers and school leaders to strive towards improving their practice. This expectation is evident in your CPD policy.					
We evaluate CPD frequently to understand what's working well, what needs to be changed during the CPD programme, and what needs improvement.					

believe in small changes. You don't have to overhaul everything at once. Continuing to do things the way we've always done regarding CPD simply doesn't cut and will not drive standards in our schools. We now have good insights into what makes good teacher CPD, and throughout the book, I have referenced some very strong literature in this area and given my spin on how we design and deliver 'high-equality CPD' in our schools compared to just offering a 'CPD' provision because we have to. I believe we've made significant progress over the past 10-15 years in how we design, plan, and implement teacher CPD, and I'm confident that things will continue to improve in the future.

When it comes to CPD in your school, how do you know what's working well, and why do you need to know this? Professional development can be a costly part of our school budget. It can sometimes also be a neglected part or an area where we try to save the pennies. The evidence we have, though, clearly shows the positive impact this has on our schools, our teachers, and our students, so for this reason, we must get this right.

Small changes, like those I've mentioned in the book, are extremely powerful. So begin by focusing on your school's specific area of CPD that isn't quite working for you. Get better at that, gain momentum, and then move on to the next area you wish to address. This might involve making better use of INSET days or allowing more time during the school day for teacher meetings and professional development. You know what needs to be done; initiate conversations with those around you. Good luck!

Appendices

Appendix 1

Case Study

Teaching and Learning Community at St. Mary's International School

Introduction

St. Mary's Primary School embarked on an innovative journey to revolutionise the teaching and learning experience by introducing a Teaching and Learning Community (TLC). This case study delves into the process, challenges, and accomplishments of creating a thriving and collaborative TLC at St. Mary's Primary School. All teachers and senior leaders participated in a Teaching and Learning Community (TLC), convening every four weeks as part of the school's professional development schedule. This scheduled time was mandatory, and all staff members were actively involved and committed to the TLC's objectives.

Background

Before the TLC initiative, St. Mary's faced challenges such as teacher isolation, inconsistent pedagogical approaches, and limited opportunities for professional development. The school's leadership recognised the urgent need for a structured platform to encourage collaboration, continuous learning, and pedagogical innovation among its educators.

Initiating the Teaching and Learning Community

1. Leadership Commitment

Mrs. Johnson, the school's headteacher, took a proactive role in spearheading the TLC initiative. She emphasised the importance of fostering a culture of inquiry, peer support, and shared learning experiences.

2. Formation of the TLC

Various committees were established to plan and execute the TLC. These committees encompassed curriculum development, professional development, and peer observation teams.

3. Teacher Input

St. Mary's Primary School organised surveys, focus groups, and staff meetings to collect input from teachers. This valuable feedback guided the design of the TLC framework, ensuring it met the specific needs and aspirations of the teaching staff.

4. Regular TLC Meetings

The TLC team convened every four weeks to promote sustained collaboration and discussion for approximately 60 minutes. These meetings served as a platform for teachers to discuss teaching, learning, and pedagogy and to share their experiences and insights.

5. Senior Team Involvement

A senior team member was appointed to oversee the organisation and coordination of the TLC meetings and activities, ensuring they remained a focal point of the school's agenda.

Implementation

1. Professional Development

The TLC provided continuous professional development opportunities tailored to teachers' needs. However, scheduling dedicated time for professional development amidst an already packed curriculum posed challenges.

2. Peer Observation

Encouraging teachers to embrace peer observation initially faced resistance due to concerns about judgment and evaluation. Senior leaders and cover supervisors (not teachers or TAs) covered lessons for this to be carried out.

3. Accountability

Each participant agreed to take two specific actions after every TLC meeting and report their progress to colleagues within the TLC. It was emphasised that this process aimed to enhance classroom practices and was feasible for all, regardless of how long they had been teaching or working in the school. A high level of support also plays a crucial role in ensuring that individuals remain accountable for the commitments they make

Outcomes

1. Collaboration and Community

The TLC successfully nurtured teacher collaboration, fostering a sense of community and a shared commitment to excellence. Teachers began regularly exchanging ideas, resources, and pedagogical best practices during their meetings.

2. Enhanced Professional Development

Teachers reported a marked improvement in the quality and relevance of professional development activities. They appreciated the opportunity to participate in peer-led workshops and benefit from their colleagues' expertise.

3. Improved Teaching Practices

Through peer observations and collaborative lesson planning, teachers embraced innovative and effective teaching practices, enhancing student engagement and improving learning outcomes.

4. Increased Student Achievement

As a result of the TLC's efforts, St. Mary's Primary School witnessed an upswing in student achievement scores and a narrowing of achievement disparities among student groups.

Conclusion

Introducing a Teaching and Learning Community at St. Mary's Primary School has catalysed significant positive change. Under strong leadership, active teacher involvement, and loyal commitment to collaboration, the school cultivated a culture of ongoing learning and improvement. The TLC enhanced teaching practices and contributed to heightened student achievement and a more tightly-knit school community. St. Mary's Primary School's experience serves as a beacon of inspiration for other schools aspiring to improve their teaching and learning environments through similar initiatives, with a dedicated commitment from every member of the TLC team. This became a key intervention for improving teaching and learning across the school and for improving school standards.

Appendix 2

Reflecting on Professional Development

Using this template, reflect on a new teaching technique you have tried recently as a result of a CPD activity you have participated in.

Action	What are you going to do differently?	How are you going to do this?	By when?
Description	What did you do?	How did your students respond to this?	What happened at the end?
Feelings	What were your thoughts while teaching?	How did your students feel?	How do you feel about how it went now?
Evaluation	What went well for you, and what would you like to improve?	What were the benefits and challenges for your students?	What will you do differently and why?
Conclusion	What will you do differently?	What have you learned?	What did you/your students do well?

Adapted from Gibbs, G. (1988). *Learning by Doing: A Guide to Teaching and Learning Methods*. Oxford: Oxford Further Education Unit

Whole-School Professional Development Plan

School Year: [Insert Year]

Autumn Term:

Theme/Topic	Target Audience	Short-Term Objectives	Long-Term Objectives	Success Criteria	Resources Needed	Follow-Up Activities	Types Evaluation
School INSET 1							

Appendix 3

PAUSE FOR THOUGHT – Agile Leadership Quick Reference

Take this as an opportunity to self-assess your agility. Push it a bit further and get two of your colleagues to do the same assessment on you. Then look back at their answers, and compare them with your own reflections.

	Tick ✓	Give an Example
I provide my staff with an opportunity to participate in school-level decisions.		
I articulate my views to others and seek out feedback before giving a final call.		
I make sure to plan regular times when I and the staff at my school can get together with other educators and teachers so that we can learn from them.		
I make well-thought-out plans, but I'm willing to modify them if need be.		
I give people leeway to make decisions based on their experience and authority.		
I accept responsibility for my missteps and discuss this with my team.		
I'm constantly learning and evolving, developing creative solutions to changing demands.		
I welcome fresh ideas without any hesitations.		
If it's beneficial for students and staff, I'm unafraid to take calculated risks.		
I'm unafraid to take calculated risks.		

Appendix 4

Planning Your Safeguarding Training: Guidance for Annual and Termly Training Example

Investing in staff, CPD holds immense importance for any school, as it not only entails a financial commitment but also requires dedicated staff time. At [INSERT NAME OF YOUR ORGANISATION], we prioritise the effective utilisation of staff time and ensure training aligns with their previous experience and the existing training your staff completes. We believe in collaborative planning and delivering customised sessions to different staff groups to achieve maximum engagement.

Teaching experience at the school: duration	1. New teachers and TAs within the first three years of teaching/working new to your school.	3. New teachers who have taught in your school for more than two years.	5. Designated safeguarding leads and their deputies. Senior leaders.
	2. Experienced teachers who are new to your school.	4. Non-teaching staff.	

Example Structure

   Session 1: Groups 1, 2, and 3 Safeguarding Basics: Addressing Common Scenarios at Our School (2 hours)
   Session 2: Group 4 – Safeguarding Basics and Effectively Safeguarding Children as a Non-Teaching Member of Staff (2 hours)
   Session 3: Group 5 – Safeguarding for Senior Leaders (2 hours)
   Session 4: Group 5 – Key Updates Plus At Least One Other Module from the Programme (3+ hours)

This approach guarantees that the training is tailored to suit the varying levels of experience within the school. Depending on their experience within your school and country, and working with children, including non-teaching staff in any session is possible.

Appendix 5

Lesson Observation Template: Generating Understanding and Raising Awareness

How Was the Technique/s Implemented	What Is Said and Done by the Teacher/S	What Impact Does This Have on Students	Follow-Up Questions to Explore with the Coaches

Appendix 6

The six-step feedback guide for post-observation coaching, adapted from Paul Bambrick-Santoyo's 'Leverage Leadership,' provides a framework for structuring lesson observation feedback.

Step 1: Praise - Narrate the Positive	Take one to two minutes to praise the teacher's success, and ask them how it felt.
Step 2: Probe - Start with a Targeted Question	Select a specific area of focus from the observation. You could ask the teacher how they used a technique, why they included these lesson outcomes, or how they used an activity or teaching pedagogy to increase students' understanding and mastery of the lesson. **Avoid, wherever possible, general questions.**
Step 3: Identify the Problem and Action Steps	Based on the coach's understanding of the teacher's situation, they can go into more detail using these four levels.
	Level 1 (teacher-driven) has the teacher self-identifying their problem, while level 2 has them answering scaffolded questions (more support). Level 3 involves presenting classroom data (more leader guidance), while level 4 has the coach offering guidance on possible solutions.
	In level 4 (leader-driven; only when other levels fail), you should directly state the area of improvement/problem. For example, you can demonstrate what you saw and what action step is needed to solve the problem. If you previously modelled in class, ask the teacher to explain what they did differently.
Step 4: Practice and Implementation	The practice stage is the time to role-play or simulate how to improve current or future lesson/instructional delivery. Start by asking if the teacher wants to be the student or the teacher.
	For levels 2-4, jump into role-play and replay the lesson, attempting to apply what has been learnt. You can be the student and act out a particular scenario. In level 4, you can also model for the teacher and then have them practice it.

(Continued)

(Continued)

Step 5: Plan Ahead	Design/revise upcoming lesson plans to implement this action. What to say: Where would be an excellent place to implement this in your upcoming lessons? Let's write out the steps in your lesson plan, worksheet/activity, etc.
Step 6: Prepare for Review	Prepare for review. Set a timeline for the follow-up to review implementation.
	What to say: When would be best to observe your implementation of this?
	Levels 3-4: I'll come in tomorrow and look for this technique. What is the best day, time, and activity to observe you implement this? (It's best to ask this now so you don't forget later.)
	Set a timeline for achieving action steps.

Appendix 7

Level 1 – Participants' Reactions Evaluation Questionnaire – Example Template

Name of CPD Course Date	
Rate each item from 1 to 5, where 1 is 'poor' and 5 is 'excellent.' If the question is not applicable, leave it blank.	
Were the programme's objectives made clear?	
How effective were the leader's instructional skills?	
How effectively did the programme hold your interest?	
Were the facilities conducive to learning?	
Were your questions and concerns adequately addressed?	
How useful will these ideas and skills be to you in improving learning?	
How would you rate the overall value of the programme?	

Was the material immediately useful? _____

What were the best aspects of the programme or activity?

What could be done to improve the programme or activity?
_____
_____
_____

What do you value most from this experience?
_____
_____
_____

From what you have learned, what will you use or do next?
_____
_____
_____

What topic would you like to see included in future programmes that would help you do your job better?
_____
_____
_____

Any other comments?
_____
_____
_____

Appendix 8

Level 2 - Participants' Learning Evaluation Questionnaire

Example Templates

Complete this section after your training day and then again a few weeks later.

Evaluating Professional Development Questionnaire

CPD topic _____ Job title _____	Date _____ Email _____
I learned that _____ _____	
What I found **most** helpful was	What I found **least** helpful was
What I would like to learn is (include any suggestions, appreciation or concerns)	

Appendix 9

Interview Questions (Post-Training)

Use This Framework to Create Your Own Interview Questions for Teachers and Senior Leaders

Level 1: Participants' Reactions

Here, questions should focus on the content, process, and context of the professional development experience.

Content

1. Were the issues explored relevant to your professional responsibility? If so, how and why?
2. Did the content make sense or not? Why do you say this?
3. Was your time well spent? Why do you say this?
4. Will you be able to apply what you have learned? Why do you say this?
5. Were you given adequate opportunities to explore the theory and supporting research behind the CPD? Why do you say this?

Process

1. Was the trainer effective and helpful, or not? Why do you say this?
2. Was the material covered relevant? Can you give examples?
3. Did the training include a variety of learning activities?
4. Was sufficient time provided for the completion of the training tasks?
5. Were the learning goals and objectives clearly outlined from the start?

Context

1. Were the facilities provided conducive to learning?
2. Was the room the right size?

3. Did the room provide an appropriate learning environment for the nature of the activities?
4. Were the refreshments provided of a good standard?

Level 2: Participants' Learning

1. What were the most important ideas you gained from the CPD experience? Why do you say this?
2. How will you try to put the ideas you have learned into practice?
3. Have you acquired new skills that will improve your ability to help students learn? If so, which skills are these?
4. Has the CPD training boosted staff morale? If so, in what ways?
5. Are you confident you can put your new learning, knowledge, and skills into practice? Why do you think this?
6. What aspects of the training were most helpful in meeting your CPD needs? Why do you say this?
7. Because of your CPD training, what else would you now like to learn?
8. Was there an appropriate balance between presentation and interaction with colleagues? If not, how could this have been improved?

Level 3: Organisational Support and Change

1. Was ample time given to meet with colleagues and to plan collaboratively?
2. Of the support given by the school, what did you find most useful during the CPD training? Why do you say this?
3. Were there aspects of the CPD not helpful or useful?
4. Has staff feedback on the CPD been shared with you? Has this been used to improve programme delivery and the support provided?
5. Do you feel CPD activity is aligned with the school's mission, goals, and objectives?
6. Can you describe what senior leaders have done to encourage and support the CPD programme? Is there anything else that could have been done or tried out?

7. During the CPD programme, did you have access to relevant resources to support you during the training?
8. Have you been encouraged to try new practices or strategies? Or are you worried about being criticised if positive results are not readily apparent?
9. Because of the CPD, is sufficient time now provided to discuss difficulties with colleagues and to develop solutions?
10. Because of the CPD, have you been offered opportunities to visit colleagues and observe their classroom teaching methods? If so, how often has this occurred, and have you had the chance to reflect on what you have seen?

Level 4: Participants' Use of New Knowledge and Skills

1. How has it been going since the start of the professional development? Are you using? What do you feel most confident about and why?
2. Has your knowledge of the subject increased? Why do you say this?
3. Are you feeling more confident compared to where you were three months ago? Why do you say this?
4. What has helped you implement and use new ideas learned through CPD training?
5. Describe what you are doing differently, if anything, because of the CPD training.
6. What are you now doing in the classroom that is different from what you did before?
7. What evidence do you have to show you are using a new approach or idea and doing something differently?
8. Has professional development raised standards of teaching and learning in the school? If so, how?

Level 5: Student Outcomes

1. Were the intended student learning outcomes made clear to you at the start of the CPD programme? If so, how were these explained to you?

2. What have you done so far to evaluate the impact of the CPD programme on student outcomes?
3. Would you say the CPD activities you participated in helped develop students' knowledge, skills, attitudes, beliefs, or behaviours? Why do you say this? If so, how will you ensure this continues to be the case?
4. What evidence could you collect to show that students have benefited from the CPD programme, such as increased self-esteem, greater engagement, or adopting a growth mindset when it comes to learning?
5. Do you think professional development has led to improvements in student achievement? Why do you say this, and what evidence do you have for this?
6. Do you feel it is fair to evaluate the professional development of educators in terms of the impact on students? Why do you say this?

Appendix 10

Example Timeframe for Carrying Out a CPD Evaluation

Adapted from Guskey's five levels of CPD evaluations

Levels	Timeframe	What Can Be Done
Level 1: Initial Reaction to the CPD	24-48 hours	Participant feedback forms Teacher interviews Focus group meeting
Level 2: Assessing What's Been Learnt	Within three weeks	Questionnaires to assess progress since the start of the CPD programme Interviews with participants as well as mentors and/or coaches Coaching meetings Learning walkthroughs Lesson observations Focused group meetings Review during departmental meetings
Level 3: Organisational Support	Within four weeks	CPD leads organise coaching meetings Teaching and learning communities Learning development walkthroughs Focused lesson observations, video observation analysis, external visits, and collaborative learning walks Staff interviews to highlight support needed (you can refer to questions in Appendix 3)

(Continued)

(Continued)

Levels	Timeframe	What Can Be Done
Level 4: Embedding Practice	Within 16-18 weeks	Teacher questionnaires/interviews Focused lesson observations Reflection journals Student questionnaires
Level 5: Student Outcomes	Within 16-18 weeks	Information on gathering evidence on improvements in students' cognitive, affective, and psychomotor developments through questionnaires, interviews, school records, classroom assessments, or external standardised assessments

Appendix 11

CPD Audit Checklist

CPD Statements	Yes ✓	No ✓	Somewhat ✓	Examples of Where This Can Be Seen	RAG Rate
We utilise research to shape the design and planning of CPD activities and programmes.					
CPD is consistently maintained over time, providing frequent opportunities for learning, experimentation, practice, self-reflection, and evaluation. Honest and frequent feedback and solutions-focused conversations are integral components of our approach.					
Our approach focuses on evidence-informed practices, challenges existing assumptions, and centres around what works.					

(Continued)

(Continued)

CPD Statements	Yes ✓	No ✓	Somewhat ✓	Examples of Where This Can Be Seen	RAG Rate
Subject-based CPD meetings are scheduled at least once a month.					
Both novice and expert teachers are provided with opportunities to collaborate and support each other.					
The entire school comes together for CPD sessions at least once every six weeks.					
Lesson observations contribute to CPD activities and serve as a means of assessing the effectiveness of practical strategies. Time is allocated afterward for productive developmental conversations, aiming to support the observed teacher in becoming even better.					
Weekly directed time is allocated for professional development activities.					

(Continued)

(Continued)

CPD Statements	Yes ✓	No ✓	Somewhat ✓	Examples of Where This Can Be Seen	RAG Rate
Formal qualifications are integrated into our CPD offerings for staff.					
Clear teaching standards are in place, providing a framework for teachers and school leaders to strive towards improving their practice. This expectation is evident in your CPD policy.					
We evaluate CPD frequently to understand what's working well, what needs to be changed during the CPD programme, and what needs improvement.					

Index

Note: Page numbers in *italics* indicate figures, and page numbers in **bold** indicate tables in the text

active listening 103, 114, 122, 125
agile leaders, skills of 49–51
agile leadership 51–52, **52**, 191
Alexander, G. 123
apathy, challenging 175–176
Ashes, L. J. 170
attentive listening 123–126
autonomy 121, 129

Bambrick-Santoyo, P.: 'Leverage Leadership' 126
Beere, J. 112; 'Grow - Change Your Mindset, Change Your' 67
behaviour change 53; four laws of 57–59
Bernes, E. 114–115
best practices, sharing 82
bite-size information 81
Briceño, E. 20
Brighthouse, Sir T.: 'The Jigsaw of a Successful School' 116
Burch, N. 71–73

Centre for the Use of Research and Evidence in Education (CUREE) 147

challenge, level of 81
challenging individuals, dealing with 102–106
change, problem with 14–16
Cheliotes, L. M.: 'Coaching Conversations: Transforming Your School One Conversation at a Time' 122
clarity/objectives, lack of 89
Claxton, G. 66
Clear, J.: 'Atomic Habits' 56, 57
coaching 110–137; effective questioning 123–126; GROW model of 123, 129; instructional 126–132, 135–137; meaningful lesson observations 132–135; mentoring vs 111; personal growth, questioning for 122; post-observation, six-step feedback guide for 194–195; principles and practices, exploring 111–113; questions, reflection on 123, **124**; questions, types of 122–123; relationships, fostering 120–121; situations 113–114; transactional analysis and 114–115

coach selection 114
Coe, R.: 'The Case for Subject-Specific CPD' 52
collaborative accountability 117
collaborative alignment 117
collaborative choice 117
collaborative partnership 126
collaborative support 34-35, 117
comfort zone 17, 55
communication 19, 50, 70, 97, 114, 115; interpersonal 111; non-verbal 125; verbal 125
competence, four stages of 71-72, 72
confidentiality 120
connection to previous learning 81
consultation stage 38-40
co-operation 121
Covey, S.M.R. 19; 'The 7 Habits of Highly Effective People' 15; 'The Speed of Trust' 17
CPD audit: checklist **179-180**, 205-207; RAG exercise **149-152**
CPD programmes 86, 88-90
critical consumers 22-24
cultural leader 17-19
culture 16-17, 120, 136
CUREE see Centre for the Use of Research and Evidence in Education (CUREE)

Deans for Impact: 'Practice with Purpose: The Emerging Science of Teacher Expertise' 54
deliberate practice 10, 53-55, 127
delivery 99-101; methods 83-84
Department for Education (DfE): Standards for Teachers' Professional Development 147-148

designing 23, 33-38, 41, 45, 88, 106, 145, 174-175
developmental approach 118
DfE see Department for Education (DfE)
didactic CPD 42, 93
disruptive behaviour 104
dopamine 66-67; impact on motivation 66
Downey, M. 112
Drucker, P. 16
duration 33, 52

educational conferences 98-99
Education Endowment Foundation (EEF) 43, 84, 147, 148; effective professional development guidance report 2021 36-38, 37; Professional Development Report 174; 'The Impact of COVID-19 on Learning: A Review of the Evidence' 13
EEF see Education Endowment Foundation (EEF)
effective professional development 31, 62-63, **61-62**; EEF report 2021 36-38, 37
egalitarianism 121
empathy 50, 103
equality 2
Erikson, T. 103
evaluation 43-44, 141-166; definition of 148, 153-154; dos and don'ts **159**; facts of 154-155; formative 155-160; Guskey's five critical levels of 160-165, 203-204; ignoring 90; impact of CPD 142-143, **159**; of organisation

support and change 162-163; paradigm shift in 165-166; of participants' learning 161-162; of participants' reactions 160-161; of participants' use of new knowledge and skills 163-164; pedagogy 144-146; planning 165; of student learning outcomes 164-165; summative 155

Evidence-Based Education: 'A Model for Great Teaching' 84-86, 87

expert teachers 9-14; qualities of 12

fear of pursuing CPD 176-177

feedback 4, 36, 49, 54, 73, 86, 88, 92-94, 96, 98, 110, 114, 126, 127, 132-135, 144, 161, 167, 177; conversation 133; external 52; formative 160; forms 143, 158; high-quality 55; ignoring 90; informative 145; mechanisms 97; meeting 134; positive 57; professional 90; summative 160; surveys 44

Fine, A. 123

focus 55

Foer, J.: 'Moonwalking with Einstein' 14

follow-up, twilights without planning 42-43

formative evaluation 155-160

formative feedback 160

Furnham, A.: 'Leadership: All You Need to Know' 18

GDPR 101

Gibbs, G.: *Learning by Doing: A Guide to Teaching and Learning Methods. Oxford: Oxford Further Education Unit* 42

goals 55, 176-177; PEERS 130; teacher 127

Grant, V. 112

GROW model of coaching 123, 129

Guskey, T. 142, 143, 159; five critical levels of professional development evaluation 160-165, 203-204

habits: attractive 58; easy to master 58; formation 53; motivation and 63-65; obvious 58; satisfying 58; stacking 59-60; tiny, power of 56-57

Hanushek, E.A. 14

Hattie, J. 10; 'Teachers Make a Difference, What is the research evidence?' *11*

Heath, C.&D.: 'Switch' 59-60

high-quality CPD 22, 172-173

high-quality feedback 55

inclusivity 2, 97, 104

informative feedback 145

INSET (In-Service Education and Training) 38, 69, 136; avoidance factors 92-93; days 90-93; essentials for 90-92; practical tips 91; running 42-43; stand-alone 92-93

instructional coaching 126-132; barriers to, addressing 135-137

insufficient support 89

interview questions (post-training) 199-202

Jeffers, S.: 'Feel the Fear and Do It Anyway' 9

Kahneman, D.: 'Thinking, Fast and Slow' 68
Kain, J.F. 14
key commitments, establishment of 82
Kline, N.: 'Time to Think' 68
Knight, J.: 'Impact Cycle: What Instructional Coaches Should Do to Foster Powerful Improvements in Teaching' 129-132; 'The Definitive Guide to Instructional Coaching' 120-121, 126
knowing-doing gap 16, 54
Kolb's reflective cycle 80
Kraft, M.A. 19, 20, *21*

learning objectives 81, 156, 162
Lemov, D.: 'Leverage Leadership' 126; 'Teach Like a Champion' 84
lesson observations 70; meaningful 132-135; template 192
Little, J. 116

management 33-34; performance 70, 133
marginal gains 53
Maslow, A.: hierarchy of needs 63-64, *63*
McKinsey & Company 15; 'How the World's Best-Performing School Systems Come Out on Top' 10; 'Psychological safety and the critical role of leadership development' 19
mental models 55-56
mentoring vs coaching 111
Merrill, R.R.: 'The Speed of Trust' 17
motivation 63-65; dopamine, impact of 66

Murray, M. B.: 'Teach Like a Champion' 84

non-verbal communication 125
note-taking 125
nudge effect 71

one-size-fits-all approach 89
online CPD 44-45, 96-98; avoidance factors 98; positive aspects of 97-98
organisation 33-34; support and change 162-163
outcomes 3, 18, 22, 26, 30, 31, 39, 60, 78, 81, 92, 99, 130, 144, 158, 164-165
oxytocin 67

Papay, J.P. 19, 20, *21*
paradigm shift 165-166
participant engagement, lack of 89-90
participants' learning evaluation 161-162; questionnaire 198
participants' reactions evaluation 160-161; questionnaire 196-197
participants' use of new knowledge and skills, evaluation of 163-164
pedagogical approach 118, 138
pedagogical discussions in meetings, promoting 69
pedagogy 11, 15, 26, 31, 53, 65, 67-69, 95, 128, 129, 131, 134, 144-146, 177
peer learning 34-35
PEERS goals 130
Pendleton, D.: 'Leadership: All You Need to Know' 18
performance management 70, 133

personal growth, questioning for 122
personal inertia 14
Pfeffer, J. 16
planning 77-106, 174-175; evaluation 165; vital components for 78-80
positive feedback 57
positive mindset 103
praxis 121
primary colours model 18
professional environment 19-22, *21*
professional feedback 90
professional learning: school environment and 69-71
purposeful activities, with focus on learning 81
purposeful practice, developing teachers through 53-56

qualitative methods 158
quality: of CPD 7, 73, 141-142; high-quality CPD 22, 172-173; high-quality feedback 55; teacher 9-26
quantitative methods 158
questions: coaching 123-126, **124**; types of 122-123

rational thinking 103
real-life practical classroom strategies 81-82
recruitment 13, 14, 23, 171
reflection 121, 189; points 82; stage 40-41
Reilly, M. F.: 'Coaching Conversations: Transforming Your School One Conversation at a Time' 122
relationship-building 18
research evidence 23-24
retention 13, 14, 23, 78, 81, 171

Rivkin, S.G. 14
Robinson, V.: 'Student-Centered Leadership' 22
Rosenshine, B.: 'Principles of Instruction' 84

safeguarding training 192
schedule, overloading 89, 93
school culture 16
school environment, and professional learning 69-71
sense of psychological safety 19
serotonin 67
sessions of professional development 93-96
simplified CPD 84-86
Sinek, S. 32
staffroom CPD 69
Standards for Teachers' Professional Development 147-148
student achievement: CPD impact on 35-36
student learning outcomes, evaluation of 164-165
summative evaluation 155
summative feedback 160
Sutton, R. I. 16; 'Developing Teachers' 31; 'What Makes Great Teaching' 31

TA *see* transactional analysis (TA)
tailoring stage 39-40
teacher appreciation 82-83
teacher collaboration 116-117, **119**
teacher goals 127
teacher quality 9-26; cultural leader 17-19; culture and 16-17; experts 9-14; problem with change 14-16; professional environment and 19-22, *21*

teacher training 2-5
Teaching and Learning Community (TLC)185-188; accountability 187; background 185; collaboration 187; community 187; enhanced professional development 187; formation of 186; implementation 186-187; improved teaching practices 187; increased student achievement 187; leadership commitment 185; outcomes 187; peer observation 186-187; professional development 186; regular meetings 186; senior team involvement 186; teacher input 186
Teachmeets 93-96
thinking environments 20, 67-68
timing 43
tiny habits, power of 56-57
TLC *see* Teaching and Learning Community (TLC)

top-down approach 41
tracking 65
training: excellent 120; programme, reading and writing **157**; stage 40
transactional analysis (TA) 114-115
trust 17-19, 34, 41, 67, 120, 134

understanding 39, 44, 50, 53, 54, 73, 78-82, 85, 94, 103, 104, 111, 114, 131, 148, 163

verbal communication 125
vision 18, 32-33, 38-39, 46, 52, 90

Whitmore, Sir J. 112, 123; 'Coaching for Performance' 122
whole-school CPD: difficulties, overcoming 101-102; plan 190; survey **146**
William, D. 84; 'Leadership for Teaching and Learning' 35

For Product Safety Concerns and Information please contact our EU
representative GPSR@taylorandfrancis.com
Taylor & Francis Verlag GmbH, Kaufingerstraße 24, 80331 München, Germany